Franco and the Spanish C

This series of introductions to widely studied and newer areas of the undergraduate history curriculum provides short, clear, self-contained and incisive guides for the student reader.

Franco and the Spanish Civil War is a wide-ranging and insightful analysis of the origins, course and consequences of the conflict and of Franco's role within it. It offers a broad view of the war through a survey of its social and cultural, as well as its military and political dimensions. In particular, it traces Franco's meteoric rise to power, his conduct of the war, and his long subsequent rule.

This authoritative introduction illuminates the many different interpretations of the conflict by examining a variety of perspectives. *Franco and the Spanish Civil War* places the war in its national and global contexts, exploring both nationalist and republican points of view, and giving attention to foreign participation in the conflict. It provides an accessible and well-rounded starting point for any student of the subject.

Filipe Ribeiro de Meneses is lecturer in Spanish and Portuguese history at the National University of Ireland, Maynooth.

Introductions to History

Edited by David Birmingham

Franco and the Spanish Civil War

Filipe Ribeiro de Meneses

London and New York

First published 2001
by Routledge
11 New Fetter Lane, London EC4P 4EE

Simultaneously published in the USA and Canada
by Routledge
29 West 35th Street, New York, NY 10001

Routledge is an imprint of the Taylor & Francis Group

© 2001 Filipe Ribeiro de Meneses

Typeset in Sabon by Keystroke,
Jacaranda Lodge, Wolverhampton
Printed and bound in Great Britain by TJ International Ltd,
Padstow, Cornwall

British Library Cataloguing in Publication Data
A catalogue record for this book is available from the British Library

Library of Congress Cataloging in Publication Data
De Meneses, Filipe Ribeiro, 1969–
  Franco and the Spanish Civil War / Filipe Ribeiro de Meneses.
     p. cm. – (Introductions to history)
  Includes bibliographical references and index.
  1. Spain–History–Civil War, 1936–1939. 2. Franco, Francisco,
  1892–1975. I. Title. II. Introductions to history (New York, N.Y.)

DP269 .D35 2001
946.081–dc21   00–45041

ISBN 0–415–23925–7 (pbk)
ISBN 0–415–23924–9 (hbk)

Contents

Acknowledgements

This book would have been impossible without the help of a number of people. Professors John Horne and Don Cruickshank, Edward Arnold, Cormac Ó Cléirigh and, above all, my wife Alison, have provided invaluable aid. To them goes all my gratitude.

Filipe Ribeiro de Meneses
Maynooth, April 2000

Extracts from Alun Kenwood's *The Spanish Civil War: A Cultural and Historical Reader* (Berg 1993) reprinted courtesy of Berg Publishers.

Every effort has been made to secure permission for copyright material. If a copyright holder has been inadvertently omitted, please apply in writing to the publisher.

Abbreviations

AP Acción Popular
CEDA Confederación Española de Derechas Autónomas
CNT Confederación Nacional del Trabajo
FAI Federación Anarquista Ibérica
FET y de las JONS Falange Española Tradicionalista e de las Juntas de Ofensiva Nacional Sindicalista
FETE Federación Española de Trabajadores de la Enseñanza
FNTT Federación Nacional de Trabajadores de la Tierra
HISMA Compañía Hispano-Marroquí de Transportes
JAP Juventud de Acción Popular
JSU Juventudes Socialistas Unificadas
PCE Partido Comunista de España
POUM Partido Obrero de Unificación Marxista
PSOE Partido Socialista Obrero Español
PSUC Partit Socialista Unificat de Catalunya
ROWAK Rohstoff-und-Waren Kompensation Handelsgesellschaft
UGT Unión General de Trabajadores
SIM Servicio de Investigación Militar
UME Unión Militar Española
UMRA Unión Militar de Republicanos Anti-fascistas
UP Unión Patriótica

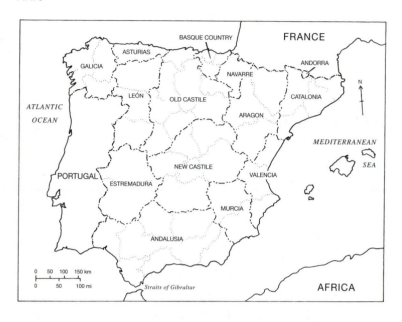

Regions (top) and provinces (bottom) of Spain
Source: Adrian Shubert (1990). *A Social History of Modern Spain*, Routledge.

The main battlefields of the Spanish Civil War, as illustrated by a 1938 Nationalist tourist brochure advertising tours of the country

Route No. 1: The North.
Route No. 2: Aragon.
Route No. 3: Madrid.
Route No. 4: Andalusia.

Introduction

The importance of studying the Spanish Civil War might seem, at least to those outside Spain, to be secondary. After all, the Spanish conflict occurred between two world wars which dwarfed it in size, scope and consequences. However, even a cursory glance at a library catalogue will reveal the interest stimulated by the war in Spain. Academics, writers, artists and cinema directors have all felt, and still feel, a strong compulsion to portray the Civil War in their work. There are powerful themes running through a conflict in which so many of the participants, both Spanish and foreign, were volunteers motivated by private political beliefs. The Spanish Civil War was a conflict marked by personal commitment, freely made, to the fighting, despite official paralysis or indecision. In the world wars men fought, for the most part, as cogs in the enormous machines of national armies, the exception being those involved in resistance movements from 1939 to 1945. The hands of the belligerent governments were behind all aspects of life for those at war, maximizing the potential of the armies at the front. The Spanish Civil War was not, in this sense, a total war, but it is worth noting that the amount of historical and fictional attention paid to resistance movements in the Second World War is wholly disproportionate to their military contribution. Although the line between civilians and combatants in Spain was blurred, the ability of the two contending governments to mobilize and discipline the resources theoretically at their disposal was limited, especially in the case of the Republic. Into this breach stepped Spanish and foreign volunteers, and their selfless gesture has not yet been forgotten. The Civil War's importance is not exhausted by the scale of individual commitment. It also played a crucial part in defining the alliance systems, the military strategies and tactics, and, at a personal level, political attitudes – the decision to resist or collaborate – that would characterize the Second World War.

A survey of the views of significant wartime figures in Spain, and of subsequent historians of the conflict, reveals the difficulty of encapsulating the Civil War in an elegant sentence or a quick, insightful and memorable explanation. It was hardly a war between communism and fascism, or between Western democracy and fascism. It was not a war of revolution versus reaction, or progress against tradition. It was evidently not a case of good versus evil. If we consider the scale and importance of foreign intervention, the very name by which we remember this conflict might be called into question. Contrasting perceptions of the war, in the 1930s and today, have generated completely different interpretations of the causes and the nature of the Civil War. At the time, and in the face of horrors that shook the rest of Europe, a cultural or racial explanation was sought for events across the Pyrenees. *The Times*, on 21 August 1936, stated that the 'appalling cruelty' displayed in the Civil War had 'betrayed the gulf between the Spanish mentality and that of most of the rest of Europe'. Irwin Laughlin, American Ambassador to Spain in the early 1930s, suggested that it was a frequently made mistake to portray the Spanish as a Latin 'race' – the Spanish nation, rather, was formed 'chiefly from the tough old aboriginal Iberian tribes of the peninsula; subdued with the greatest difficulty by the Romans; mixed with the rough Visigothic blood which infiltrated from the north . . . and subjected then to the strong cultural influence of the Moors'. The result was that 'the mass of the Spanish race today is, true to its blood, a hard, resistant, vigorous and pugnacious strain, highly individualistic with a touch of fatalism, not over-sensitive to pain either physical or mental' (Keep the Spanish Embargo Committee: 19). In Spain itself the interpretations were many and varied. The Nationalists described the war as both an attempt to forestall a communist revolution and a crusade for Western civilization and the defence of Christianity. Leading figures of the Republic, naturally, saw matters differently. Indalecio Prieto, of the Spanish Socialist Party (PSOE), claimed that 'this war, which started as one for liberty, has turned into a war of independence' (Spanish Embassy 1937: 45). Not only was the Spanish Republic fighting internal rebels; it was fighting the combined strength of Germany, Italy and Portugal. A link was thus established between the events of 1936–9 and the popular rising against Napoleon's army in 1808. André Marty, commander of the International Brigades, described the war as 'the basis for a revolution which will rid Spain of its semi-feudalism and its age-old obscurantism' (Marty 1937: 33). In other words, for the communists the war was the process by which the bourgeoisie's historical mission in Spain – the creation of a true parliamentary democracy – was finally being accomplished, not by the bourgeoisie itself but, instead, by a mobilized and disciplined working class.

In the aftermath of the Second World War, as tension between the West and the East mounted, the war was increasingly explained in terms conditioned by the Cold War: it had been, if not necessarily motivated, then at least usurped, prolonged and worsened by Moscow. Communists had seized power in the Republic through underhand means and had forced the rest of the Republic's defenders to fight, according to the communists' terms, for longer than they should have. The Cold War also permeated the writings of Spanish exiles. Without access to sources, and enduring the hardships of their prolonged absence from Spain, their written accounts of the war became bitter and personal polemics which did little to aid the Republic's cause. The first attempts at an overall and, as far as possible, impartial account of the war thus fell to foreign scholars, who tried to piece together events on the basis of these personal accounts, the press and foreign archival sources. More recent scholarship, Spanish or otherwise, has bypassed these personal, political and exploratory phases, examining an ever wider array of sources in the search for a better understanding of both the causes of the conflict and the true dynamics that existed within each of the rival coalitions struggling for mastery of Spain. There is still considerable disagreement among historians, however, on many subjects pertaining to the Spanish Civil War, notably in their attempts to provide figures for both combatants and victims.

Spain was not allowed to forget the war until the 1970s. Francisco Franco's control over his country was founded upon total victory. For nearly forty years the memory of the war was kept alive by the winning side in order to justify its hold on power. This was a divisive memory of the conflict, one in which the victors were impossibly good and virtuous and the defeated the sum of every vice and perversion, traitors sworn to destroying their country against whom full vigilance had to be maintained – the kind of vigilance that only Franco could provide. In Spain the war was for decades explained as an attempt by the army to thwart a Masonic and communist plot, attention being focused on the anticlerical outrages of 1936. The end of the Francoist regime and Spain's transition to democracy have helped the historian's work enormously, allowing Spanish scholars to participate openly in the debate over the Civil War while making available a much greater range of documents. Further archival collections have been opened to historians in Russia, to where party and government papers were removed by some of the Republic's fleeing supporters.

The interest that the Spanish Civil War has subsequently generated in terms of personal accounts, novels and films remains strong. In 1995 the film *Land and Freedom* was released to wide acclaim and popularity, showing once again that the Civil War is regarded with fascination. In the Spanish language alone over 900 novels related to the war have been published. The experiences of those who participated in the war, and who had come from all over the world, were transformed into poetry, diaries, fiction and film. The quality of the literature generated by the Civil War can rival that of any major historical event of the twentieth century. The sense of injustice and urgency of a war perceived to be about ideas and progress rather than outright national interest was a powerful catalyst for artistic creation. The list of authors who visited, fought and wrote in and of Spain is enormous and unique: W.H. Auden, John Cornford, Stephen Spender, Louis MacNeice, George Orwell, Erich Arendt, Bertolt Brecht, Gustav Regler, André Malraux, George Bernanos, Franz Borkenau, John dos Passos, Ernest Hemingway. Many of the books written at the time, and still thought of as classics, were clearly works of propaganda, in which artistic individuality was subsumed into a wider cause. The attraction that communism held at the time for intellectuals, in part due to its desire to fight, alone if necessary, the spread of fascism, made this process easier. Other works managed to convey a different point of view, in which unease with the Republic's future was mixed with an admiration of those who, on the ground, fought and died for it. Orwell's *Homage to Catalonia*, of these, stands as the most popular and perhaps the most moving.

It seems fitting, given the quality and breadth of recent research into the Spanish Civil War, to provide newcomers to the subject with a new introduction to the study of the conflict. This work approaches the Spanish Civil War from a variety of angles, supplementing more traditional political and military analysis with a consideration of relevant social and cultural factors. Because of its nature, it necessarily draws on the work of other historians, notably Ronald Fraser, Helen Graham, Stanley Payne, Paul Preston and Adrian Shubert. Nevertheless, primary sources are also referred to. The Civil War's origins, its course and the way that it was experienced by both Nationalists and Republicans are explained, as are Franco's meteoric rise to the top of the Nationalist hierarchy, his conduct of the war and the consequences of his military success for the future of Spain. Each chapter of this book attempts to serve as an introduction to its respective topic and as a bridge to further reading.

CHAPTER ONE

The origins of the Spanish Civil War

The ferocity with which the Spanish Civil War was fought astounded a Europe still recovering from the shock of the First World War and in which the victors of 1918, Italy excluded, were anxious to preserve the peace that followed. The war in Spain, which lasted for thirty-three months, resulted in half a million deaths and constituted, for a time, the focal point of European politics. Spain suddenly abandoned the periphery to which a slow decline had condemned it, becoming the centre of attention for world powers which moved with care in order to achieve their goals without provoking a major confrontation. Victory in the Civil War would also provide the sustaining myths for the dictatorship of Francisco Franco, which lasted until the Caudillo's death in 1975. As the scale of losses indicates, the commitment of both sides to the fighting was great and sustained. Any examination of the Civil War must begin with the origins of the conflict, which, as this commitment to the fighting suggests, are to be found in diverse spheres: social, economic, cultural and political.

1.1 SOCIETY

Spanish society, at the turn of the century, was marked by considerable inequalities, the result of very different patterns of socio-economic development. At intervals throughout the nineteenth century Spain was torn by internal strife, usually between the Carlists, defenders of traditional monarchy and a predominant social role for the Catholic Church, and those who wished to implement more liberal ideas. This conflict hastened, as can be expected, the decline of the country, whose international prestige had already suffered a tremendous blow with the independence of most of its Latin American colonies at the start of the century. The realization of this lack of prestige, and of what it meant in practical terms, took a long time to sink in. The final shock of defeat at the hands of the United States, in 1898, was needed for the state of the country to be fully appreciated, and then only in a mood of panic. Cuba was Spain's prized colony, but the failure to reach a compromise with an increasingly assertive independence movement led to war and the eventual military intervention of the United States, by then looking for colonies of its own. Spain's army and navy were comprehensively defeated by more modern American forces, a humiliation made harder to digest by examples of corruption and incompetence that marred Spain's war effort. Spain's last remaining colonies – Cuba, Puerto Rico and the Philippines – were lost. In the space of four years, 200,000 soldiers were sent from Spain in her vain bid to retain a colonial empire. Because exemptions from military service could be bought even in times of war, it was the poor who suffered most from the conflict. The Spanish–American War highlighted both Spain's military and diplomatic weaknesses and the need for radical change if Spain was once again to pursue successfully her interests on the international stage. This change could be made by moving either to a truly democratic constitutional framework, which might tap into the country's energy and human potential (a revolution from below), or, conversely, to a more authoritarian and nationalist solution which would sacrifice political and even economic liberty for the sake of order and progress (a revolution from above). The political debate that ensued attracted Spain's leading intellectual figures, collectively known as the 'Generation of '98', who made public their gloom and despair, adding a tone of urgency to the need for a solution to be found but finding little practical response to their calls for reform from either the public or the state.

Part of this gloom and despair grew from the fact that Spain's economy, seemingly backward and rural, did not appear capable of generating the wealth required to close the gap with the more developed powers of Europe. Spain was, however, poised for an important industrial leap forward, which was to come as a result of the First World War. Economic development in Spain, though rapid in the early twentieth century, would retain its uneven course, with serious consequences, as we shall see, for the fate of the Second Republic in the 1930s. In its infancy, Spanish industry had been essentially dependent on foreign capital, mostly British and French, which began to arrive in the second half of the nineteenth century and which was directed towards the development of a railway network and mining, the latter concentrated in the region of Asturias but with other important centres throughout the country. By the turn of the century two main centres of Spanish enterprise had developed.

In the Basque Country metallurgy had emerged as a leading industry, attaining an important level of concentration and modernization; by 1900 there were 22,000 metalworkers in the city of Bilbao.

Basque industrialization attracted immigrants from the rest of Spain, whose numbers, poverty and different language and customs hurried the development of Basque nationalism. In Catalonia, meanwhile, the traditional manufacture of textiles had survived due to mechanization and concentration throughout the nineteenth century. By 1892, the textile industry employed 70,000 workers, mostly in Barcelona itself, attracting labour from the province and later from the whole country. Althought this Catalan textile industry had been dependent on the captive market provided by the colonies, it was able to withstand the shock of the 1898 defeat. The loss of the colonies, nevertheless, led to the realization by Catalan politicians that the central power in Madrid did not view their immediate concerns – economic or cultural – as a priority. The fact that the two centres of modernization and industrialization in Spain were the capitals of provinces seeking to restore their traditional autonomy exacerbated tensions within Spain. The struggle for regional autonomies and the preservation of their distinct languages was successfully presented as a drive for liberation from the corrupt, poor and backward remainder of Spain. Madrid's industry was essentially limited to food processing and consumer goods, and was characterized by smaller factories or workshops.

By 1900, Spain boasted 76,000 miners, 706,000 workers in manufacturing of all sorts, and 236,000 construction workers. These numbers, however, accounted for a mere 13 per cent of the workforce. A change in official mentality towards industrialization took place after 1898, when Spain's technological backwardness was so dramatically demonstrated. Import substitution by domestically manufactured products was suddenly identified as the key to economic renewal and industrial reform. In 1906 tariff protection was extended to industry in order to protect it from foreign competition, and this device was to be increasingly resorted to throughout the first half of the century. Finally, it must be mentioned that the increases in the numbers and the social and economic importance of the industrial working class were accompanied by an ever-greater syndicalist presence. Unions grew quickly, thriving on the difficulties encountered by the workers in dealing with employers. The most important unions were those with anarchist and socialist affiliations; others, including those of Catholic inspiration, were much less important numerically.

Spain was, as a result, an agricultural country with 60 to 70 per cent of its labour force employed in the primary sector. Nearly half of the population of 18.5 million lived, before the First World War, in villages of less than 5,000 inhabitants. Nevertheless, the country was divided into several totally different systems of land ownership. The *minifundia*, extremely small holdings typical of the northwest region of Galicia, ensured a conservative devotion to the land and to established order, as well as a constant migration to the cities and emigration to the American continent. The south of the country – the regions of Andalusia and Extremadura – was dominated by the *latifundia*, huge estates often controlled by absentee landlords. For the owners of these estates, there was no incentive to introduce technological improvements because of the availability of a cheap labour force. Landless labourers were hired on a daily basis and had no guarantee of work even in harvest time; they could only look forward to around 200 days of work per year, outright misery being experienced during the rest. There were some areas in Spain where middle-sized farms were the norm, especially Navarre and the Basque Country. These family farms were considerably larger than those of Galicia and allowed for a more confident and assertive peasantry. Where there was widespread irrigation, as was the case in Valencia, citrus plantations also allowed for profitable and stable family holdings. In Catalonia, agrarian problems were to be found among the *rabassaires*, who rented the land on which they grew their vines. Traditional periods of rental no longer matched the life of the vines planted after the ravages of phylloxera in the nineteenth century, provoking widespread instability. The land-owning peasantry of northern Spain, however much land it owned, was generally conservative, Catholic and firmly opposed to any talk of land reform which might entail the distribution of land to those that had none. Despite the often appalling poverty of landholders in Galicia, property owners all over Spain banded together in defence of their right to own land, so that the owners of the vast estates in the south, many of whom controlled the greatest fortunes in Spain, could be assured of a mass following in their opposition to land reform.

The existence of these different landholding arrangements had been determined by Spain's distant past – notably the Reconquista – and by developments in the nineteenth century, which had not witnessed any significant land reform, but merely the state's expropriation of much of the Catholic Church's land, sold to the highest bidder. The Church's land was thus acquired by existing landlords, whether or not they were members of the nobility, and wealthy city dwellers looking for investment opportunities. Once-liberal financiers, merchants, professionals and officials, having invested in land, thereafter adopted the outdated social attitudes of the traditional landed class. In this way a new rural elite was created which, mixing old and new money, dominated the country's economic and political life, preventing any rural reform and progress.

It is impossible to give an overview of Spanish society at the beginning of the twentieth century without considering the role of the Catholic Church. In the nineteenth century the Church in Spain was the target of attack by liberals who sought to curtail its privileges, expropriate its land and break its hold on politics. In the face of the social change that shaped the nineteenth century, the Church was at a crossroads: it could seek accommodation with the new circumstances through a series of internal reforms, or could react against those circumstances. It took the latter route, attempting to halt all social and political progress at a time of great inequality. The result was that the Church lost the allegiance of both the new urban workers and the landless labourers. It chose to emphasize charity by the wealthy and the maintenance of order over the need for reform to alleviate the hardship of the poor.

One of the successes of Spain's constitutional monarchy in the latter half of the nineteenth century was that it harnessed the Catholic Church to the needs of the state while curbing both its independent intervention in politics and its considerable economic influence. It did so by protecting the Church from further liberal attacks. In Spain the relationship between Church and state was controlled essentially by the Concordat of 1851 and the Constitution of 1876. Initially forbidden, non-Catholic religious practices were tolerated after 1876 only if held in private. The Crown had the right to appoint bishops and the secular clergy was maintained by the state, one-seventh of the national budget being fixed for this purpose. The Church was nevertheless allowed to own property, and a limited number of male and female religious orders could operate in Spain. All education conformed to Catholic doctrine. In 1900 Spain had 33,000 secular clergy, 20,000 regular clergy and 42,000 nuns. The Church played a vital role in education at all levels, from primary to university, and it possessed a powerful press which, by 1891, numbered 248 publications, including 35 daily newspapers. In this press liberalism was identified as the cause of all that had gone wrong in the country, and further deviations from old customs, it was argued, would merely lead Spain further down the road to damnation, which could only be avoided by allowing the Church to maintain its pivotal role in society.

Despite this position of apparent strength, after its compromise with liberal reformers, the Catholic Church in Spain encountered great difficulties at the beginning of the twentieth century. The first of these was an irregular presence across the country. The rural south was being lost to the Church, and the failure to respond to the rapid urban growth of such cities as Barcelona was significant. In the Catalan capital in 1909 there was only one priest for every 10,000 workers, for new parishes were simply not being created. Rural priests were both badly paid and educated, and one of the consequences of the earlier sale of church property by the liberal governments was that the Church was made dependent on the state and on rich benefactors for its income. It was less able than in previous eras to take up the cause of the dispossessed or ameliorate their distress. According to the Spanish Church, inequality was divinely ordained, and poverty and wealth were spiritual tests for both rich and poor. These theories were defended from the pulpit, in the press and in religious schools and seminaries. The antipathy towards the Church among workers grew and was seen in incidents such as the 1909 Tragic Week in Barcelona, when 21 churches and 31 monasteries were burned down in the city, although clergymen themselves were spared. Despite this catastrophe, the Church did not develop any real sense of a social mission. The Uniones Populares – the Church's attempt to establish Catholic trade unions – failed to attract any significant support as a result of their paternalistic attitude to labour relations.

A partial consequence of the Catholic Church's role in society was the standing of women who, unsurprisingly, and broadly in line with the rest of Europe, were victims of discrimination. If single at twenty-three, a Spanish woman could sign contracts and conduct her own business, although she remained barred from political life. Upon marriage, however, she lost important legal rights, and her husband was entitled to administer all of the couple's property, including what had belonged to her prior to marriage. Disregard for the husband's authority could lead to short jail terms. Inequality within marriage was also present in relation to adultery, considered to be a crime, since crimes of passion committed by wronged husbands carried a much lighter sentence than those committed by wronged wives. Moreover, adultery was judged to exist in all cases involving married women, but only if it caused 'public scandal' in cases involving married men, and it also carried differences in jail terms for men and women. This inequality in terms of sexual morality was further enshrined by the continued legal status of prostitution, a trade heavily regulated by the state, which had instituted a system of routine medical checks and health cards for prostitutes. Feminist organizations existed, but theirs was, for the moment, a lost voice. Divorce was unavailable in Spain until 1932; women's education, when available, served to curb expectations of future independence. Middle-class women were educated in the cult of domesticity and were not prepared for a career. In Spain, the number of women in the workforce fell in the period of 1877–1930. Although this statistic did not apply to the urban and rural working classes, it must not be assumed that socialist trade unions at the time favoured outright equality; syndicalists had, as their aim, better wages for men in order to allow them to provide for their families' total needs. They also hoped that as women returned to the home more jobs would be created.

Until 1931, and despite frequent calls for reform from both the left and the right, little was done to overcome the basic fact that Spain made for a shocking contrast with the leading powers in Western Europe. The poor, especially in the south, were in an almost unique situation. They owned no land to cultivate, were completely dependent on their respective landlords for the ability to work, enjoyed no form of social protection, and had to endure the presence of a sizeable and ruthless police force – the Guardia Civil – whose essential duty was to keep them in order. As the twentieth century wore on, moreover, one means to escape these conditions – emigration to the Americas – was closed as a result of the Great Depression. Internal migration to Spanish cities in search of regular work was another source of relief, but the amount of labour that could be absorbed by Madrid, Barcelona, Bilbao and other large cities was limited. This scale of poverty had many consequences, a self-defeating one being the limits it placed on the market for Spanish manufactured goods. Few people could afford them in Spain while they were too expensive to compete abroad, and so the growth of Spanish industry, on which the country's modernization depended, was strongly restricted by domestic poverty.

In the cities, workers could count on increasingly powerful unions to defend their interests, be they the socialist UGT (founded 1888) or the anarcho-syndicalist CNT (founded 1910). The latter, a mass anarchist movement, was a uniquely Spanish phenomenon. The often incompatible ideals of Russian anarchist theoreticians Mikhail Bakunin and Peter Kropotkin were combined with more recent syndicalist theories emanating from France to create a world view in which the state, in whatever guise, was described as the ultimate enemy of the people, and in which the essential virtue of the individual, once released from the bonds of capitalism, was equally affirmed. The CNT had as a goal, therefore, the substitution of the state and its agents by trade unions and collectives capable of negotiating directly with one another, exchanging goods and services in order to meet all the needs of the population. Whether these trade unions should be organized as local units, or as more powerful national associations, was a frequent source of contention within the movement. By 1918, it is estimated that the CNT, strongest in Catalonia and the rural south, had over 700,000 members, although its actions were hampered by disagreements over ideology and tactics, since it was hard to instil collective discipline in a traditionally individualistic movement. The struggle for improved working conditions, higher pay and the preservation of existing jobs could not be dissociated from internal and external factors: the continuous migration from other areas of Spain, which allowed employers to set low wages; the struggle for political influence of the Basque and Catalan bourgeoisie, whose interests generally played second fiddle, in terms of national politics, to those of the large landowners; and the structural weaknesses of the Spanish economy, whose industry found it hard to compete with its European rivals, leading to great insecurity in the workplace. Foreign events such as the First World War and the Russian Revolution also had great impact on labour relations in Spain, the first allowing for an economic boom – accompanied by increased social tensions as prices rose higher than salaries and new fortunes were amassed – and the second providing workers with an example of what could be achieved through concerted and determined action in a country that was still largely agricultural.

1.2 POLITICS

Spanish society was undergoing a process of clear fragmentation in the first decades of the twentieth century. The forces that had kept Spain together in the past were losing their prestige while nothing was taking their place. The authority of powerful entities such as the Catholic Church, the monarchy and the armed forces was no longer accepted unquestioningly. The armed forces were hamstrung not only by their poor performance against the United States in 1898, but by the subsequent disastrous war in Morocco, which culminated in the 1921 disaster of Annual, the greatest single defeat of a European army by an African force. Over 8,000 Spanish soldiers perished and thousands more were captured.

The monarchy, finally, was discredited as a result of the political practices prevalent in Spain. Under the constitutional monarchy, elections were not the means by which popular political will was measured – by which, in other words, popular sovereignty was exercised. Elections to the Spanish parliament, the Cortes, were instead the means by which existing governments legitimized their rule. There were two main parties, Liberal and Conservative, nominally different but essentially sharing the same broad outlook and thoroughly corrupted by the rotative system. Whenever a crisis occurred, or some financial scandal made it impossible for the existing government to continue in place, the monarch (Alfonso XIII after 1902) would summon the opposition party to form a government. Once in power, this government would call an election and, without fail, obtain a victory, thereby governing peacefully until the next crisis. The ability of successive governments to obtain the desired electoral result, in peaceful rotation, was built upon the action of the *caciques*. A *cacique* was a local notable, the most powerful man in any given rural constituency. His main function, from the central government's point of view, was to arrange electoral results in accordance with the intended outcome. To this end, the *cacique* would occasionally resort to force and intimidation, but he usually worked in more subtle, and corrupt, ways: distributing patronage and promises, finding employment in the civil service and local administration, and bringing improvements to the constituency, in order to buy votes. In return for this service, his authority in the area went largely unquestioned, whether or not he served in an official capacity. Parties were merely loose coalitions of figures with ill-defined programmes rather than vote-winning machines competing against each other; campaigning was largely unheard of. It was often the case that only one candidate presented himself in a given constituency, as a result of which no election had to take place. The implications of the system were immense. The machinations of the *caciques* became equated, in the minds of the rural population, with the parliamentary system. This facilitated the growth in popularity of anarchism, which denounced all political activity as innately fraudulent and, conversely, gave traditionalist ideologies such as Carlism a longer lease of life than was the case with equivalent philosophies in the rest of Europe. Moreover, the renewal of ideas and views at government level became impossible. The interests of a narrow and essentially rural oligarchy were perpetuated, with obvious implications for the social and economic development of the country. It was virtually impossible for other views to be represented at national level, and so a disparity began to emerge between the real strength of competing socio-economic groups and their ability to influence national politics.

The system was practically immune to reform, being vulnerable only in the larger cities where a disciplined left-wing (socialist or radical) or regionalist vote existed. Despite its resilience, the rotative system was obviously insufficient either to deal adequately with the challenges facing Spain or, increasingly, to preserve power in the hands of the ruling oligarchy. Constitutional politicians found it difficult to preserve the balance of power which so favoured them while dealing with new problems for which they were unprepared and which released political passions that were impossible to contain. The most significant of these problems were the First World War, which divided political opinion into interventionist and neutralist while having a massive impact on Spain's economy, and the unpopular war in Morocco, but even lesser crises could throw Spanish politics into turmoil. In 1917, for example, middle-ranking officers came together in the Juntas movement to prevent a proposed reform of their service which threatened the principle of promotion by strict seniority; successive governments found themselves unable to stand up to the officers effectively, revealing the limits of political authority. That same year the constitutional monarchy was also threatened by a general strike and an attempt by reformist politicians to create an alternative parliament, free from the influence of the two largest parties; both of these initiatives were thwarted, but the danger for the rotative system had been real. The system was also unable to provide solutions for deeper structural problems such as the continuation of poverty, illiteracy and discrimination against women, or the growing power of the trade unions during and after the First World War. Finally, there was a clear need to devolve some power to Catalonia and the Basque Country, the richest and most modern regions in Spain, or even just to give their respective industrial and financial bourgeoisie a greater say in the decision-making process in Madrid – yet here as well little action was taken. The paralysis seemed complete.

The years 1918–21, misleadingly known as the *trienio bolchevique*, saw a string of anarchist revolts in the south as landless peasants, driven by the dream of abolishing the large estates and replacing them with communal land ownership, rose in revolt. To this rural strife were added clashes in Barcelona between workers and employers, with violence and counter-violence between, on the one hand, anarchist gunmen and, on the other, employer-sponsored assassins, the Carlist Sindicatos Libres (used essentially as strike breakers), the police, and a militia force, the Somaten. With the end of the First World War came the realization that Spanish industry was still unable to compete with its European rivals, finally released from the obligation to produce war-related items. As employers began to cut their labour forces to make savings, the unions reacted angrily. Between 1917 and 1923 there were over 1,000 political murders in Barcelona alone, and the scale of the violence left Catalan business interests doubtful about the desirability of political reforms leading to a genuinely democratic system. Government and parliamentary inertia in the face of mounting crisis was the norm, because politics rested not on proper representation of the national will but on an ever-weaker parliamentary fiction. By 1923 it had become clear that the system could not survive any longer. Confronted by two options – genuine reform, turning Spain into a true democracy, or a dictatorship – the King opted for the latter, welcoming the coup led by General Miguel Primo de Rivera in that year.

Primo de Rivera, fifty-three years old when he seized power, was met by conflicting expectations of what a dictator should achieve in Spain. The first set of expectations revolved around the defence of privileged interests. For many at the time, Primo de Rivera was in power simply to deflect attention from the issue of responsibility for the disaster at Annual, which threatened the military chain of command all the way up to the King; to fight against the CNT, destroying its ability to defend workers and throw Catalonia into turmoil; and to protect the Catholic Church and private property, including the *latifundios*. In other words, from this point of view the dictatorship had been established to carry out the basic function of the monarchy since the 1870s – keeping a lid on reform – but in a more aggressive fashion made necessary by the strain of new social and economic pressures. As a member of the landowning class of southern Spain, these tasks came naturally to Primo.

The second set of expectations involved the notion of the 'iron surgeon', first advanced by Joaquín Costa, a reformer writing in the aftermath of 1898. The iron surgeon was a dictator who, imbued with full powers, could carry out the reforms that successive parliaments and governments had endlessly discussed but not accomplished: the modernization of Spanish industry, the expansion of road and irrigation systems, the reform of the armed forces and the education system, and the improvements in the life and working conditions of the urban and rural proletariat, leading to its smooth reintegration into the national whole. From this point of view, the dictatorship had been created to bring Spain resolutely into the twentieth century. This was agreeable to an army officer, always conscious of his country's standing among the other powers, and Primo relished this side of his task. His reformist zeal was exemplified by the decision to work with both employers' organizations and the socialist UGT, led by Francisco Largo Caballero, in the search for good labour relations. The two sets of expectations, which Primo tried to reconcile, were, however, clearly contradictory, and the enterprise failed. True reform was impossible without the abandonment of privilege, and Primo could not square this circle.

Ultimately, Primo de Rivera was not sufficiently brutal or devious to quell the mass of opinion that emerged against his continued rule, and his attempt to create a single party, loosely modelled on the Fascist experience in Italy, the Unión Patriótica (UP), collapsed under the weight of its lack of purpose, direction and initiative. Primo was successful when the international economy was buoyant and Spain could borrow the capital needed to finance massive public works and irrigation schemes, the development of new industries and the creation of a university complex in Madrid. However, few structural reforms were carried out and when the economic conditions turned sour in the late 1920s the days of Primo's rule were numbered: José Calvo Sotelo, his gifted finance minister, found it impossible to increase direct taxation in the way necessary to pursue Primo's plans. The truth was that Spain's privileged minorities did not consider Primo's role as reformer and modernizer to be more important than his role as defender of their interests and were not willing, as a result, to fund his programmes with higher taxes on their wealth.

Primo de Rivera, in the space of seven years, made too many enemies. Alfonso XIII, previously the lynchpin of the rotative system, was jealous of the dictator's power. Politicians were no longer assured, as before, of profitable sinecures. Army officers felt threatened by Primo's intended military reforms, which included, inevitably, promotion by merit. Intellectuals were angered by censorship and the arbitrary treatment of universities, in whose life Primo interfered. Businessmen could not accept the inclusion of the UGT as a true social partner, and were shocked when arbitration tribunals found in favour of the workers. Finally, the CNT resented its continued repression and became even more militant after the creation, in 1927, of the hardline FAI, a secret organization whose goals were the preservation of the CNT's anarchist principles and the refusal of any constructive contact with the state.

1.3 THE SECOND REPUBLIC, 1931–3: REFORM AND LEGALITY

Although desired by Alfonso XIII, the fall of Primo de Rivera was a terrible blow for the King. Primo's dictatorship had represented the monarchy's last gamble to remain relevant, and the subsequent dictatorial government under General Dámaso Berenguer could do little to halt the spread of republican sentiment among the population of the large cities. The growth in republicanism was fostered by the ill-advised execution of Captain Fermín Galán and Lieutenant García Hernández, two officers implicated in a failed republican rising in the town of Jaca, not far from the French border. This new political mood manifested itself openly in the 1931 municipal elections. After hearing the first counts, which demonstrated a massive republican victory in the cities, the King and his advisers, without waiting for the full results, decided to leave the country as quickly and as quietly as possible, handing power over to a shadow government made up of civilian republican politicians. The Second Republic was born not out of revolution, but of the disintegration of monarchical authority, although its arrival was welcomed throughout the country by popular demonstrations. The new Republic, when it appeared, was bathed in optimism, and there seemed to be a universal acceptance of the government's reform programme. This, however, was a deceptive impression, for conservative opinion had not disappeared. It had merely – and momentarily – lost its voice.

In 1931 there was no political leadership articulating the views of Spain's privileged elite. The old monarchist parties had disappeared during Primo de Rivera's dictatorship, which was eager to distinguish itself from their inefficient rule, and time would be needed to form new parties capable of forging an alliance of all property holders, great and small, to fight the republican reforms. Without this conservative voice being heard, politics naturally swung to the left, and in its early months, as a Constitution was drafted and the first laws were passed, the Republic quickly defined its personality and proclaimed its goals. Spain was to be a genuine democracy, political life ridding itself of the influence of the *caciques* once and for all. She was to be a secular country, all ties between the Church and the state being cut, and the Church's leading educational role being curtailed. The action of the Republic would not be limited to the political life of the country, for the Constitution committed the regime to work for the economic, social and cultural well-being of all of its citizens. To this end the state would have the power to divest the wealthy of their property, provided compensation was paid. Labour Minister Francisco Largo Caballero and Justice Minister Fernando de los Ríos, from the earliest days of the Republic, introduced legislation designed to correct the intolerable situation in the countryside. They ensured that labour could not be brought in by a landlord from outside the municipality in which his property was located; an eight-hour working day was introduced; cultivation of productive land was deemed obligatory (an imposition designed to create employment in rural areas); leases were made practically permanent and rents were frozen; and tribunals representing both landowners and workers were created in order to resolve remaining disputes at local level. Largo Caballero was thus ensuring the continuation of his tactics during the

Primo de Rivera years, using the UGT's collaboration with the state to weaken the CNT and establish a syndicalist monopoly for the socialists. Greater equality was also to be produced by the enfranchisement of women, a significant reform guaranteed by the 1931 Constitution. Finally, at regional level, provision was made for the devolution of power to Catalonia and the Basque Country, whose special identities within the Spanish nation as a whole were recognized. Devolution to a Catalan government, the Generalitat, occurred in September 1932; the Basque Country, where the situation was more problematic, would have to wait until the outbreak of the Civil War to gain autonomy. It was the intention of the republican government, moreover, that all of these goals be accomplished within the strictest obedience to the law. Power, in other words, should not fall to the street, as was demonstrated by the repression of CNT strikes and insurrections.

Many problems were to plague the Republic's short existence, some of which were beyond the control of its leadership. In the first place, the Republic came into being at a time when democracy was on the retreat across Europe. Confronted by the triumphant communism of the Soviet Union, or the dictatorships of Portugal, Austria, Italy and Germany, the republican programme looked outdated: it was setting out to do, essentially, what had been done in France after the Dreyfus Affair, and proposed by the First Republic in Portugal in 1910. Second, it came into existence at a difficult time for the world economy – in the middle of the Great Depression – with high tariffs across Europe, barriers to internal emigration and low agricultural prices, all of which had a serious impact on Spain, whose agricultural exports were vital to its economic well-being. The changes proposed by the republicans might have been more easily accepted had the economy been booming.

Domestic difficulties also plagued the republican leadership. The anarcho-syndicalists remained in place, denouncing the new regime as they had renounced its predecessors and preaching, as before, immediate violent revolution – but this time benefiting from the greater freedom provided by the Republic in order to operate more effectively. Their actions, such as the seizure of power and subsequent establishment of libertarian communist societies in the towns of Llobregat in January 1932 and Casas Viejas a year later, as well as repeated strikes, did much to destabilize the Republic and undermine its leaders. Cyril Connolly, in a celebrated article, described the libertarian communist vision of Spain: 'A Spain in which the work and wealth is shared by all, about three hours' work a day being enough to entitle anyone to sufficient food, clothing, education, amusement, transport and medical attention' (Kenwood 1993: 64). It was very difficult for the new Republic to compete with this vision, or even to accommodate it. There was not enough money in the government's coffers to purchase land from its owners for social redistribution, a factor aggravated by a flight of capital from the country. By the end of 1933, less than 5,000 people had been settled on land provided by the Institute for Agrarian Reform. Redistribution of land, therefore, remained a distant mirage for the majority of landless labourers, whereas all landowners, large or small, saw it as an immediate threat. The fact that the Guardia Civil often chose to side with the landlords rather than impose government decrees made tensions worse.

One of the most salient, and controversial, aspects of the early years of the Republic was the anticlerical nature of its legislation. The entire Spanish left was united in its desire to reduce the Church's power and influence in a dramatic fashion. For the republicans, anticlericalism was a way of attracting immediate mass support for the regime without delivering more controversial and divisive social reforms. The attack on the Church began in 1931, before the first general election was held, despite the doubts of the provisional government's leader, Niceto Alcalá Zamora. Along with the interior minister, Miguel Maura, Alcalá Zamora was a Catholic committed to the creation of a positive relationship between the Republic and the Church. The provisional government turned its back, however, on the religious provisions of the 1876 Constitution and the Concordat. Religious freedom was proclaimed, as was the regime's rigorously secular character. The Church's control over education was the target of much legislation. Religious teaching was limited and religious imagery was removed from classrooms; at the same time, qualifications that ruled out most clergymen involved in education were demanded from teachers. Even the Church's ability to dispose of its property was suspended, raising fears of a forthcoming confiscation of buildings and works of art. The Constitution, when approved, made reconciliation between Church and state much more difficult. Article 26 confirmed Spain as a secular state, wherein no church received the financial support of the Treasury, and allowed the Catholic Church two years' grace to prepare for the change.

Article 48 proclaimed the principle of a unified, and lay, education system. The Society of Jesus was dissolved while legislation covering the running of other orders, which were not allowed to teach, was promised. Divorce was granted, cemeteries were submitted to civil jurisdiction, and public demonstrations of faith, such as processions, were deemed to require official approval. The Church's reaction was made public in a pastoral letter published on 1 January 1932, in which the Spanish prelates outlined what the attitude of Catholics to these measures should be: intervention in politics to defend religion and country, acceptance of the constituted order but not of legislation opposed to the laws of God and the Church, participation in public campaigns for church education and the defence of the Catholic institution of marriage, and support for the Catholic press.

The legislative attack on the Church could be justified from a legalistic point of view, but its political wisdom was, at best, dubious, alienating as it did middle-class Catholics eager for political reforms but not at the expense of their faith. Conservative smallholders in central and northern Spain were also horrified. Worse still, for all Catholics, was the government's inaction in the face of a spate of attacks on church property in May 1931, which saw over one hundred religious buildings throughout the country sacked while the police forces were restrained by the government from intervening, and the expulsion from Spain of two prelates – the Bishop of Vitoria, Mateo Múgica and the Cardinal of Toledo, Pedro Segura – in circumstances of very doubtful legality. The campaign against the Church, and the failure to prevent violent acts against religious property, accelerated the mobilization of conservative forces, including the creation of a mass conservative coalition, the Confederación Española de Derechas Autonomas (CEDA), capable of defeating the left in the race for votes. CEDA, described as *accidentalist* (which is to say that it was willing to use the Republic's institutions to implement its programme), had at its heart the Acción Popular party of José María Gil Robles, a committed political Catholic increasingly dazzled by authoritarian successes elsewhere in Europe. Gil Robles understood that the threat of agrarian reform and the treatment of the Church made possible the mobilization of rural smallholders against the Republic and launched a furious campaign to capture their support. To the right of CEDA stood the so-called *catastrophists*, who believed the nature of the republican regime to be fundamentally flawed and regarded its destruction as

17

their priority. Among them stood the followers of Alfonso XIII, grouped in a party misleadingly known as Renovación Española, the Carlists and, eventually, the Falange, Spain's version of the Italian Fascists.

1.4 THE SECOND REPUBLIC 1934–6: ACCIDENTALISM AND CATASTROPHISM

All of the political forces loyal to the Republic were badly divided among themselves, and there was no stable mass republican party. The Republic's leading statesman, Manuel Azaña, aged fifty-one in 1931 and prime minister since October of that year, had to be included on a socialist ticket in order to be elected to parliament in 1933 because his own party, Acción Republicana, was so weak. Other republican parties, including the Radical Party led by Alejandro Lerroux, disputed the middle-class electorate, but the supporter of the regime that garnered most electoral backing was the PSOE. The socialists were not, however, completely convinced by Azaña's path of orderly and gradual reform. Fearful of inroads into their popularity by other left-wing forces, such as the anarchists or the Partido Comunista de España (PCE), they sought to hurry the transformation of Spanish society, especially in relation to land reform. Disagreements between the socialists and mainstream republicans, compounded by splits between the various factions of the Socialist Party (especially those headed by Indalecio Prieto and Francisco Largo Caballero), would allow the right back into power in 1933. Prieto, more moderate, was committed to working with the republicans to carry out the reforms he identified as essential for Spain; Largo Caballero was more restless, fearing that inaction might lead to the erosion of UGT support in favour of the CNT.

In 1933 President Alcalá Zamora, who as a conservative republican was angered by Azaña's views on the Church, quickly grew disillusioned with the regime for which he was partially responsible and in which he held the highest office. He resolved the mounting political crisis by dissolving the Cortes and calling for fresh elections. The result was a shock for the left, whose control over politics passed to the centre-right and right because of two factors: an electoral law which favoured wide coalitions (in each province 80 per cent of deputies were assigned to the party, or coalition, with most votes) and the anarchists' refusal to endorse the Republic. CEDA, whose campaign was richly funded, burst on to the political scene with great success, benefiting from the split between republicans and socialists who, short-sightedly, did not form an electoral coalition. Power passed to the Radical Party, led by Alejandro Lerroux, whose government was supported by CEDA. Lerroux, aged sixty-nine, was a historic figure in Spanish politics, a revolutionary firebrand in the early years of the century who, with age and the growth of the Socialist Party, had moved steadily across the political spectrum. He and his party were also the targets of constant, and often justified, accusations of corruption. In order to keep political power and the immediate privileges it conferred, Lerroux had to pursue a conservative policy, for his government depended on CEDA's goodwill for its survival in parliament. All of the reforms initiated two years earlier, including the secularization of schools and land reform, were brought to a halt as employers and landowners reasserted their primacy. Once again Spanish politics were in stalemate, a condition unacceptable to those who conceived the Republic to be the answer to that inertia, a regime in which badly needed reforms could be carried out while at the same time law and order were maintained. Tensions mounted accordingly, with the anarcho-syndicalists carrying out yet another failed rising in December 1933, strongest in the Aragonese capital, Zaragoza. Problems were exacerbated by a strike, the following month, of the Federación Nacional de los Trabajadores de la Tierra (FNTT), the UGT-affiliated union of rural labourers, which resulted in the imprisonment of the union's leadership. Thousands of other arrests took place alongside the closing of workers' centres. These tensions reached a climax on 26 September 1934 when Gil Robles decided that, as the largest party in the country, CEDA should be represented in government.

The true nature and intentions of CEDA have remained a source of controversy among historians. The party borrowed the political trappings of fascist groups, including the appellation *Jefe* for Gil Robles and uniforms for its youth wing, the Juventud de Acción Popular (JAP), and its leaders spoke of the coming moment when they would impose their ideas on the government. Yet, when the time came to do so, they hesitated to take the law into their own hands. A series of fascist-inspired rallies caused apprehension among socialists, who proceeded – the usually realistic Prieto included – to import arms, mostly without success. In October 1934 Lerroux bowed to pressure and allowed CEDA into the cabinet, a move which, considering CEDA's size, was not unexpected. CEDA was given three portfolios reflecting its central concerns: Labour, Justice and Agriculture. The left immediately rose against the government in a poorly planned fashion. There was a failed general strike in Madrid which, being Largo Caballero's stronghold, was a source of great embarrassment for him; a violent rising in Asturias, where dynamite-wielding miners formed a revolutionary committee and seized power; and, most incredibly, a declaration of independence within a notional Federal Republic of Spain by the president of the Catalan Generalitat, Lluys Companys. This rising was to prove a disaster for those who engaged in it. The army, using troops ferried from Africa, regained control of Asturias, where anarchists, communists and socialists made a common effort to resist, in a bloodbath that cost over 1,000 lives; Catalan autonomy was suspended; and thousands of workers, alongside leading socialist and republican figures, were arrested or forced to flee abroad. Labour conditions, especially in the countryside, were allowed to worsen further. This being the case, Gil Robles, war minister by May 1935, had the country at his mercy, but chose to continue to respect the constitutional order, first being denied the position of prime minister by a distrustful Alcalá Zamora, then accepting the president's decision to dissolve parliament early in 1936, and, finally, fighting a new electoral campaign. These were crucial months for the Spanish right. Its various currents, along with the army, were unable to come together in order to define a common project, to establish a clear hierarchy, and to impose their will on the rest of the country. This failure would have dramatic implications for political developments in the Nationalist camp during the Civil War.

If in 1933 the electoral law had functioned to the advantage of the centre and the right, in 1936 it worked to the benefit of the Popular Front. This was the name adopted by an alliance between moderate republicans and those to their left – socialists and communists (the PCE having increased its visibility by taking credit for the Asturian rising, benefiting from imprisoned socialist leaders' denial of any involvement in the violent events of October 1934) – which also received a significant boost from anarchists, voting to secure the release of political prisoners from jail. As with its French counterpart, the Spanish Popular Front was an attempt by parties committed to the preservation of parliamentary democracy to ward off the threat of fascism. The Popular Front emerged triumphant from the elections of 6 February 1936, and Manuel Azaña returned to the leadership of the government. In an increasingly violent atmosphere the radical Republic reasserted itself, while in the south the spontaneous occupation by agricultural workers of large estates began. Catalonia's autonomy was restored, and the debate over the Basque Country's status began anew. Educational reforms were also restarted. Gil Robles's star waned as Calvo Sotelo, Primo de Rivera's finance minister, returned from exile to lead the monarchists of Renovación Española. Attention was also focused for the first time on the actions of José Antonio Primo de Rivera, son of the former dictator. José Antonio had formed a fascist-inspired party, the Falange, in 1933, which he committed to violent action in the struggle against Marxism. Its numbers swollen with members of the JAP, angry over CEDA's fall from power, the Falange rose to prominence with a series of violent actions which aimed to destabilize the political life of a regime which conservative Spain was no longer willing to tolerate. So serious a threat did the Falange become that it was outlawed and its leadership, José Antonio included, arrested.

At the same time, and on the left, Largo Caballero was placing further pressure on the government by claiming that he was not prepared to wait any longer for the social reforms that the country needed and that any means were legitimate in the construction of a socialist state. Dubbed the 'Spanish Lenin' by his supporters, the socialist leader, who had willingly collaborated with the Primo de Rivera dictatorship in the 1920s, was now legitimizing, through his speeches, violent action against a democratic regime and against conservative interests, even if, ultimately, he was not committed to carrying out a revolution. Such violent action was taking place in the south, where labourers were seizing estates, taking for themselves what agrarian reform had failed to deliver. Largo had been radicalized in recent years by CEDA's threat to the UGT and, more specifically, to its largest component, the FNTT; in his bid to put pressure on the regime he even opened negotiations with the PCE for the reunification of the two parties. The communists unilaterally dissolved their own small trade union, and the fusion of the youth wings of the two parties into the Juventudes Socialistas Unificadas (JSU) took place in April. In the midst of the social crisis, meanwhile, republicans and socialists, instead of seeking to provide unity and firm leadership, devoured each other. President Alcalá Zamora was vindictively dismissed from his post by the left-controlled Cortes, and replaced by a reluctant Azaña, who then saw his first candidate for prime minister, the capable and energetic Indalecio Prieto, vetoed by the parliamentary membership of the PSOE, led by Largo Caballero. This terrible series of political miscalculations saw the most popular and effective republican leader, Azaña, promoted to a position of little actual power and his most trusted ally, Prieto, prevented by his own Socialist Party, at open war internally, from becoming the PSOE's first prime minister. The resulting government, led by Casares Quiroga, a republican, was weak, and inspired little trust in either the right or the left.

Political violence escalated throughout this period, spiralling beyond the control of the government. A long series of tit-for-tat murders culminated on 13 July with the kidnapping and assassination by left-wing police officers of José Calvo Sotelo who, in the wake of CEDA's defeat, had become the most outspoken defender of conservative interests in parliament. This was to be the event that triggered an army coup to destroy the republican regime, an action whose rapid failure would result in the Civil War. The dream of a Republic capable of carrying out, in the space of a few years, the reforms which had eluded the monarchy in its various guises had come to an end, and the people of Spain were soon to face the consequences.

CHAPTER TWO

The Spanish army and the rise of Franco

The officers who rebelled against the Republic's government in July 1936 had many historical precedents for their actions. It was nothing new for the Spanish army to intervene forcefully in politics. It had done so regularly throughout the nineteenth century, and during the constitutional monarchy the army enjoyed such power and influence that, for the most part, it did not need to make public its wishes in order to see them realized. When it did intervene, either to protect its corporate interests through the Juntas movement of 1917 or, with Primo de Rivera's coup, to put a lid on allegations of corruption and incompetence in the prosecution of the Moroccan campaign, the army revealed openly the extent to which it saw itself as the legitimate embodiment of national interest.

Recent years had not been easy for the Spanish army. Defeat at the hands of the United States in 1898 had left officers with a crisis of morale on their hands and a thin-skinned sensibility that brooked no questioning from any quarter in Spain. This state of affairs was worsened by continual difficulties in Morocco, where a decisive victory that would bring peace to the troubled protectorate seemed beyond the army's ability. Handling such an authoritarian and protective military force was to prove beyond the ability of the Republic's leadership.

2.1 THE SPANISH ARMY FROM MONARCHY TO REPUBLIC

The Spanish army in the first third of the twentieth century saw itself as a caste apart from the rest of society, and without a doubt most of its officers shared a number of basic political beliefs that made intervention in the country's public life acceptable in their eyes. Army officers were, as a rule, nationalist, conservative and authoritarian. This unanimity of opinion, not present in the nineteenth century, resulted from a number of factors. First and foremost was the embarrassment over the defeat at the hands of the United States, and the resulting search for an explanation (necessarily, for reasons of pride, outside the armed forces), which led rapidly to the conclusion that the civilian politicians, by allowing Spain to fall behind her rivals, had made defeat inevitable. Second, the increasingly loud voicing of regionalist feeling in the Basque Country and Catalonia, and the assertion of internationalist beliefs by working-class organizations, seemed to officers to be an indication that their country was falling apart under the pull of foreign ideas which civilian politicians could no longer contain. The long and costly war in Morocco helped to accentuate this feeling of isolation, with the army committed to an 'honourable' solution to the conflict which might then herald a resurgence of Spain as a military and imperial power, while many politicians on the left, such as Alejandro Lerroux, saw it only as an open-ended commitment whose sole beneficiaries were officers looking for rapid promotion and investors in Moroccan mines. By 1909 there were 40,000 Spanish soldiers in Morocco, and public anger over conscription had led to the Tragic Week in Barcelona, when 120 people were killed amid scenes of rioting and military repression. An old-fashioned appeal to patriotism had worked during the Cuban War and in 1898, but the circumstances of the resulting defeat, the embarrassment suffered by the state on that occasion and the lack of any major concessions in the intervening years meant that working-class civilians resisted conscription for Morocco, clashing directly with the army's plans. Third, there were material issues at stake. The Spanish army was traditionally top heavy, with far too many officers for its size. This led, on the one hand, to the impossibility of modernization as a result of an enormous payroll and, on the other, to the impossibility of promotion by merit, with the notable exception of the *africanistas* – officers serving in Morocco – who had access to promotion as a result of actions in battle. There was a generalized feeling among officers on garrison duty in Spain that their colleagues in Africa were breaking ranks by accepting such promotions. Field exercises and refresher courses for officers were ignored, and many officers in Spain had a second job to supplement their meagre salaries. The absence of material comforts was compensated for by secure employment, the cult of patriotism and contempt for civilians held responsible for the army's woes.

Miguel Primo de Rivera's seizure of power in 1923 seemed to promise the style and content of politics to which Spanish officers had, for so long, looked forward. Despite having established good relations with the Catalan bourgeoisie while based in Barcelona as captain-general, Primo reined in all regionalist ambitions. Establishing a solid working relationship with the socialist trade union, the UGT, in the hope of eventually integrating the working classes into national life, he persecuted its anarcho-syndicalist rival, the CNT, which insisted on the need to fight the state in all its guises. Ambivalent about the merits of the war in Morocco, where political and religious resistance to Spanish designs had led local leader Abd el-Krim to proclaim the independence of a Republic of the Rif, Primo was nevertheless fortunate to benefit from French intervention in the war against Abd el-Krim in 1925. Coordinated action with French forces allowed the Spanish to achieve the honourable victory longed for by the *africanistas*, reconciling them to the rest of the army. Primo also resolved the financial difficulties of thousands of officers by employing them in national and local administrative positions. These arrangements were not stable, however, and when Primo's rule fell apart under conflicting political pressures and a mounting economic crisis the army, disorientated, was left unable to react in unison to the Republic that rapidly came into being in 1931.

This situation changed extraordinarily quickly, and the army's discontent with the new regime increased with similar speed. Officers feared that the ultimate aim of the military reforms being introduced by Manuel Azaña, the Republic's first war minister, was the abolition of a professional military in Spain and its replacement by a militia system. Azaña, in fact was, trying to reduce the army's wage bill in order to make it a more effective and modern force capable of defending the country. Committed to a strong Spanish state, he merely wanted a depoliticized army loyal to the Republic and the principles on which the new regime was built. Azaña allowed thousands of surplus officers to retire on full pay, a generous offer which was taken up by many who would, in their newly found free time, conspire against the Republic. He also, and unwisely, decided to reopen the wounds concerning the *africanistas'* rapid promotion, appointing a review board to decide upon their validity. The board's did not reach a decision for over a year, causing much consternation among those affected by the measure. Officers were further alarmed by the attack delivered by the Republic against the unitary conception of Spain to which the army had been committed for so long. Regional autonomy was granted to Catalonia despite a unilateral and unhelpful declaration of independence by the Catalan nationalist leader, Colonel Francesc Macià, and a similar project was being discussed in relation to the Basque Country. Other causes dear to the army were under threat. The CNT, an enemy of long standing, was operating openly, and the increasingly militant working class was asserting itself as never before; the Church, too, was under attack, and even the right to property was being questioned, with land reform under discussion and eventually approved. Finally, the army's right to try alleged offences against itself or the state – an authoritarian device which had long muzzled the press's ability to question any aspect of the army's existence – was abolished. It was not just the army that was alarmed by these developments. Those conservative sectors of society, which in post-First World War Italy, for example, had sought to harness the brutality of Mussolini's Fascist movement for the defence of their privileges, turned, in Spain, to the army, seeking to find protection from the challenge which the Republic seemed to pose. For them Azaña's ideal of a politically neutral army was nonsensical – as it was for many officers who had chosen to remain in their profession.

2.2 CONSPIRACY

The army first rose against the Republic in 1932 when General José Sanjurjo led an ill-fated coup in Seville. Sanjurjo, who had commanded the Guardia Civil in the past, resented his present command of the less powerful Carabineros (Spain's border guards). Blocked initially by a general strike in the southern city, the coup resulted in Sanjurjo's eventual arrest. Disorientation was still widespread in the officer corps, as it was, indeed, among the Spanish right in general, and Sanjurjo had acted in the vain expectation that fellow officers would follow his lead. His failure did not precipitate further risings because of CEDA's electoral triumph in 1933. There seemed no need for the army to intervene on the political scene because the new government was sensitive to its concerns. The army responded in kind by its thorough repression of the 1934 strikes and the subsequent rising in Asturias.

All of that changed in 1936, when the Popular Front emerged triumphant from the general elections. Suddenly, all the army's worst fears seemed about to come true. Azaña was back in power, Largo Caballero was hailed by his supporters as the 'Spanish Lenin', political prisoners arrested in 1934 were released, and a sudden move by the government to disarm and disband the army was widely discussed. The change in government was felt immediately by the army. Politically suspect generals were removed from positions of power in Madrid: Francisco Franco was sent to the Canary Islands, Emilio Mola to Navarre, Manuel Goded to the Balearics, and Joaquín Fanjul was removed from active service. All the top positions in the capital were given to generals thought to be loyal to the Republic. Before Franco left for his new post, a meeting of senior officers was held at which a coup was agreed upon in principle if any of the following circumstances arose: a governmental dissolution of the Guardia Civil or dismissal of army recruits, a leftist armed rebellion or a premature coup launched by a garrison due to a misunderstanding. Only a minority of senior officers was clearly anti-republican, and most of these were *africanistas*. All, however, were concerned with the prospects of a left-wing revolution and the restoration of regional rights in Catalonia, as well as the imminent concession of similar rights to the Basques. In 1933, middle-ranking officers had come together to form the Unión Militar Española (UME), a secret conservative organization dedicated to preparing a rising against the Republic and maintaining communications between like-minded officers across Spain. There was also a minority of officers loyal to the radical conception of the Republic defended by the Popular Front; these came together in the Unión Militar de Republicanos Anti-fascistas (UMRA). This organization, intended to counteract the UME, was open to membership from all ranks, and supplied instructors to the socialists' informal militia.

The Falange, whose influence and ambition expanded in the aftermath of February 1936, set up, on 16 March, its own military committee of friendly officers, almost all of whom were already in the UME, which was also expanding rapidly (a circular at the end of March claimed that nearly half of all active officers were now members of the UME). Another focus for a potential rising was Navarre, where a Supreme Carlist Military Junta was created. Its retired officers, by mid-March, had their own plan for rebellion. A plan by some of the more moderate officers involved in the UME to carry out a coup with the support of the outgoing president, Alcalá Zamora, failed when the latter refused to be involved.

It was at this stage that Emilio Mola took centre stage. Mola brought a new professional edge to the conspiracies. He was determined not to squander any opportunity to crush the left as he thought Gil Robles had done. By the end of April, Mola, having contacted local UME officers, was sketching the plans for the future rising. By bringing the exiled Sanjurjo into the conspiracy, having promised him a personal military dictatorship, Mola turned his plot into the central conspiracy to which other competing plots had to give way. Mola knew the rising had to be carefully coordinated, correctly estimating that it would have to dispose quickly not only of the government but also of the unions. What the conspiracy lacked was political direction: officers could agree on what they opposed – Azaña's increasingly radical Republic – but not what should replace it. To avoid splits, the rising envisaged by Mola would be controlled exclusively by the army, and it would not aim at the restoration of the monarchy, but rather at the establishment of a conservative and authoritarian Republic in which the army would have a veto over policies while remaining outside of the domain of civilian politicians, and in which the working class's independence would be curtailed. Mola was able to secure a promise of collaboration from Calvo Sotelo, Gil Robles (who gave orders for party members to support the rising and whose party funds were put at Mola's disposal), the Carlists and, eventually, the Falange. The murder of Calvo Sotelo by the police was the event that secured much of the rising's support. That the leading figure of the right in the Cortes should be murdered by the forces loyal to the government seemed to suggest that an open season had been declared against the opposition. Conservative deputies abandoned parliament in protest at the murder, and the killing of Calvo Sotelo decided wavering minds, allowing Mola to rely fully on the Carlists and the Falange as well as on a much greater number of officers than before, including, vitally, Franco.

2.3 THE RISE OF FRANCISCO FRANCO

Francisco Franco Bahamonde's life has been the subject of a number of studies in recent years, ranging from reminiscences of family members and collaborators to detailed academic works. Biographies of Franco first began to appear during the Civil War as part of the attempt to provide the Nationalist cause abroad with a charismatic and appealing leadership figure, capable of placating doubts over the legitimacy of the 1936 rebellion. What these wartime biographies made clear from the start was Franco's military pedigree. Edward Lodge Curran, in *Franco: Who Is He? What Does He Fight For?*, presented Franco as a warrior for Western civilization who had acted to prevent a communist plot from taking control of Spain and whose leadership had instantly inspired thousands of Spaniards to die for his cause, battling against Russian and French invaders of their country. Pointing out that Franco's birthplace was El Ferrol, in the province of Galicia, Curran stated that Franco was, naturally, 'warm blooded and enthusiastic and engaging' (Curran 1937: 29) – the reverse, in fact, of the stereotypical image of the Gallego, which is that of a reserved and cunning individualist. The Republic, Curran wrote, was ungrateful to this military hero of the Moroccan campaigns, closing down a military academy which he was proud to head and leaving him with plenty of time on his hands: 'Fortunate for him that he had become a man of books and a man of discipline as well as a man of action' (ibid.: 32). Franco's readings had awakened in him, according to Curran, a strong sense of social justice, putting him on the side of peasants, workers and the poor in general, and Franco acted against the government only when it had lost all legitimacy, failing to protect its citizens from 'Red Terror'. The final picture of Franco from this most charitable of American authors showed a personality cult in the making:

> He is humble, courageous, courteous and intelligent. He is calm in the face of fire. He is quiet in the face of popular demonstrations. He is forgiving to his enemies. He is beloved by the Spanish people. He belongs to them. Spain for the Spaniards! Social justice for all! This is his message. By it he stands. Because of it he cannot fail.
>
> (Ibid.: 47)

Little of this picture was in fact true, apart from Franco's status as a war hero whose reputation was built during the Moroccan wars. Recent authors have been scathing about Franco as an individual, even outside the realm of politics; one has even deemed it impossible for a biographer to make Franco interesting.

Francisco Franco was born on 21 April 1892 into a family with traditions in the administrative branch of the Spanish navy. His desire to enter the navy thwarted by cutbacks to the fleet in the aftermath of the 1898 war, Franco opted instead for the army, entering the infantry academy in Toledo in the summer of 1907. His studies were completed in June 1910, and after an initial posting in El Ferrol Franco's transfer request for Morocco was accepted in February 1912. Once in Morocco, Franco sought to be at the heart of action in order to secure the rapid promotion which the protectorate afforded, so different from the slow rise in the hierarchy typical of garrison duty in Spain itself. In the spring of 1913 Franco asked for a transfer to the Regulares Indígenas – Moorish troops fighting on the side of the Spanish – which were viewed by Madrid as expendable, usually being placed at the forefront of attacks. By February 1914, and after a number of displays of courage under fire, Franco had been promoted to captain. Three years later, despite a severe stomach wound, he had become a major at the age of twenty-four. In 1918, back in Spain, Franco met José Millán Astray, another *africanista* officer, with whom he discussed the possibility of a Spanish foreign legion based on the French model. When, in June 1920, Millán Astray offered Franco the job of second in command of just such a force, Franco accepted. The legion was formally established on 31 August 1920 as the Tercio de Extranjeros. Franco, like Millán Astray, understood that colonial wars should not be fought by the regular army, but rather by professional units and local contingents, so as not to upset domestic public opinion through casualties among young untrained conscripts. Only professional soldiers, moreover, should fight and win a dirty war, a conflict in which atrocities were commonplace and terror was an accepted weapon. Franco set no limits to the atrocities his men could commit: terrorizing the civilian population, the *africanista* officers thought, was a necessary component of victory in the Moroccan campaign. Franco's career in the foreign legion continued through the Annual disaster in 1921 to the landing at Alhucemas Bay in September 1925, the final large-scale military action conducted by the Spanish army in the Moroccan War. On 3 February 1926, by which time he had published his memoirs and been made a gentleman of the King's Chamber, Franco was promoted to brigadier general – the youngest in Europe at the age of thirty-three. In January 1928, by royal decree, Franco was made the first director of the Academia General Militar, which grouped in a single institution the army's four military academies, in Zaragoza, which he turned into an *africanista* bastion.

The years of the Republic provided a series of setbacks for Franco and the *africanistas*. General Berenguer was arrested for his role as Primo de Rivera's dictatorial successor, as was Mola, who had served as Berenguer's director general of security. On 3 June 1931 Azaña, now war minister, created a board to review promotions earned in battle. From the point of view of the *africanistas*' morale this measure was a devastating blow. Worse still was the order to close the military academy at Zaragoza, which left Franco personally aggrieved. His bitter and disrespectful farewell speech to the academy earned him a severe reprimand from his political superiors and left him without a posting for eight months. The cloud of suspicion around the *africanistas* intensified when, on 26 August, the Cortes empowered a Responsibilities Commission to investigate political and administrative offences in Morocco, political repression in Catalonia from 1919 to 1923 (including a series of murders of opposition figures), the dictatorships of Primo de Rivera and Berenguer, and the Jaca court-martial which had sentenced Fermín Galán and García Hernández to death. Franco's relationship with the Republic, however, was more complex than this inauspicious beginning might suggest, and his star moved more to the ascendant even before the right's return to power. In February 1932 Franco was finally given a posting, being sent to La Coruña as commander of the XV Galician Infantry Brigade, which he refused to commit to Sanjurjo's poorly planned uprising.

In 1933, as a result of the promotion review board's recommendations, Franco was dropped from first to twenty-fourth in the list of brigadier generals, but he was compensated for this demotion the very next month, being assigned to the Balearic Islands as military commander, a post usually reserved for major generals. In March 1934 Franco was indeed promoted to major general, becoming, once again, the youngest man of his rank in Spain. By that time he had already rejected an offer from Alejandro Lerroux to become war minister. It was in this year, as a result of the Asturias rising, that Franco made his first real mark on mainland Spain, coordinating the crushing of the rebellion. Franco assigned the worst of the fighting to Moorish troops and the foreign legion, brought over especially from Morocco; he also ordered the bombing and shelling of working-class districts in what was an extremely bloody campaign, during which the terror tactics developed in the colonial war were, for the first time, applied to Spaniards. As a reward for his services – and with the intention of keeping Franco in charge of the ablest units in the Spanish army – Lerroux, as war minister, made Franco commander-in-chief of the military forces in Morocco. Franco's star continued to rise when Gil Robles became war minister and subsequently appointed him chief of the General Staff. In this role, Franco devoted himself to undoing Azaña's reforms and purging the army of republican officers. Although he did not react violently to CEDA's removal from government by President Alcalá Zamora, Franco did try to have martial law declared as the February 1936 electoral results became known, succeeding only in Zaragoza, Valencia, Oviedo and Alicante. Complete martial law across the country might have allowed the army, in the name of public order, to reverse the popular verdict handed down through the elections, a hypothesis which raises important questions about Franco's actions and intentions at that critical moment.

The return of Azaña to power was not a personal disaster for Franco. He was assigned to the Canary Islands as commanding officer, a post worthy of a man of his rank. However, having grown used to power in Madrid, he saw the posting as a demotion. From that moment Franco became involved in the conspiracies being organized by officers such as Emilio Mola, José Varela, Joaquín Fanjul and Luis Orgaz, all agreeing that Sanjurjo should head the rising when it came. Under strict surveillance by the police, his correspondence tampered with and his phone being tapped, Franco remained in touch with, but uncommitted to, the conspirators – to such an extent that other officers began to despair of his attitude. It is hard to gauge exactly what Franco's intentions were at this time. As late as 23 June he wrote an extraordinary letter to the prime minister, Casares Quiroga, warning him that the army was hostile to the Republic, but that it was not too late to make it loyal once again. Appointments should not be made on the basis of officers' political convictions, and the prime minister should seek the support of officers in tune with the army's 'true' mood. In the letter, eventually published in *The Times* on 7 September 1936, Franco was, in an indirect fashion, offering his services as war minister to a republican government. It was only on 13 July, when Calvo Sotelo was shot, that Franco committed himself wholeheartedly to the rising.

A brief sketch of Franco's career leaves us only with the idea of an extremely ambitious man capable of both reckless courage on the battlefield and careful intrigue, mixing loyalty to his fellow officers with undisguised political ambition. General Jouart, a French officer addressing a conference entitled *The Spanish Tragedy* in April 1938, attempted to provide a deeper understanding of Franco. To an audience predisposed to the Nationalist camp, Jouart described, in glowing terms, the man he had first met while serving as military attaché in Spain, in 1935. Franco was a small man of few words. Well set, broad-shouldered, yet agile and elegant, he had a piercing and direct gaze and a demeanour which suggested a perfect moral –physical balance, evidence of a keen sportsman. He was a devout Christian, a good family man and, above all, a 'true military intellectual' who pondered his choices at length before acting decisively (*La Tragédie Espagnole* 1938: 15). On the field of battle his courage was legendary and had made him an object of veneration in all Morocco. And yet we know that Franco was ruthless, not charitable, towards his enemies, both in Morocco and in Asturias; he permitted his soldiers to commit atrocities in the hope of provoking a panic among the enemy; his meteoric rise, when combined with his ability to emerge alive from so many battlefields and with the Spanish army's broad conception of its political role, had nurtured a messianic streak in him; and he had long harboured political ambitions. Franco initially allowed his name to go forward in rerun elections in 1936 when, after the Popular Front's triumph, some of the results of the general election were deemed null and void. He also discussed, on a number of occasions, the possibility of becoming war minister. We also know that the frequent depiction of Franco as an intellectual was largely a propaganda construct, encouraged by his own vanity. Franco read little and most of his political readings consisted of anti-communist diatribes; his world-view was built on the back of discussions with like-minded fellow officers. By 1936 he was resolutely anti-communist, anti-parliamentarian and anti-Freemason; it is nevertheless difficult to establish what, precisely, he believed in, apart from the army's right to intervene in politics and the need to replace Azaña's Republic. Certainly, the manifesto he issued on 17 July 1936 leaves us with little understanding of his political beliefs. According to Franco, as he joined the military rising, Spain was being attacked by 'revolutionary hordes who obey the orders of foreign governments', and the only forces capable of halting them were the army and navy, despite having been the victims of a prolonged campaign of 'obscene and slanderous attacks'. In the manifesto Franco stated that the Constitution, and its guarantees, had been disregarded by the country's enemy, but did not identify the Constitution itself as a source of problems. The manifesto ended with an appeal for support from the people in order, 'for the first time in the history of our Motherland . . . [to] create a reality of the trilogy – and in this order: fraternity, liberty, and equality' (Kenwood 1993: 56–8). Confusion over Franco's intentions remained in place for some time. For months after the rising the British Foreign Office, for example, believed that Franco's intention was to establish a traditional military dictatorship, and not a state closely modelled on the fascist powers.

2.4 THE COUP OF JULY 1936

Plotting for the July coup was led by General Emilio Mola, who had learnt the lessons of Sanjurjo's failed rising in 1932. For Mola, civilian support and the use of terror as a weapon were essential components of the rising, necessary in order to prevent the coordinated reaction of the Republic's supporters. If their leadership was decapitated, for example, trade unions could not declare a general strike. Sanjurjo had merely hoped that the Carlists in Navarre would rise in support of his initiative, but Mola had developed direct and concrete links with them: their militia, the Requeté, would provide an instant army in the north of Spain. A deal was also clinched with the jailed Falangist leader, José Antonio Primo de Rivera, which would further bolster the number of civilian volunteers fighting alongside the army rebels. Other leading plotters included Colonel Juan Yagüe, commander of the troops in Morocco, and General Queipo de Llano, commander of the Carabineros. Franco, despite being a household name as a result of his exploits in Morocco and the crushing of the miners' rebellion in 1934, and despite being considered a potential enemy by the Republican government, was not involved in planning at this stage of the operation. He thought, correctly, that a revolt would turn into an extremely bloody affair with an unforeseeable outcome. He preferred to wait and see. The government, led by the Galician politician Casares Quiroga, was aware of plotting within army circles, but was too weak to act, since it could not count on the support of any considerable part of the army against the conspirators. Franco, as we have seen, was in fact playing a double game, offering his services to the government while aware of the plot being hatched. After many hesitations, and after his suggestions were turned down by the executive, Franco joined the plot, but he was not earmarked for a prominent political role. The head of state after the coup was to be General Sanjurjo, exiled in Portugal; Mola, who masterminded the coup, was expected to take as a reward an important government position; and other field commanders had more important and dangerous tasks than Franco; they too needed to be compensated. Lastly, civilian politicians such as José Antonio Primo de Rivera and Calvo Sotelo would be needed to gather civilian support for the rising. Franco, it seems, aspired in 1936 to be governor of Morocco, whose forces he was to take over and command as soon as the rising took place. His subsequent rise would be due to circumstances well beyond his control, but which would again reinforce his sense of being an instrument of providence.

It was the garrison in Morocco which, fearing imminent arrest, rose first against the Republic, on 17 July 1936, a day earlier than planned. Yagüe and his fellow conspirators quickly captured the cities of Ceuta, Melilla and Tetuán. By the time Franco landed in Spanish Morocco, having already seized power in the Canaries on the morning of 19 July, the protectorate was firmly in rebel hands. The coup failed to take Spain by surprise, however, and resistance was immediate. The rising met with success in Navarre, as expected, where the Carlists, eager to destroy the 'godless' Republic, turned out in force. It was also successful in the CEDA heartland of Castile and Leon, where the Church's influence was strong: Burgos, Salamanca, Zamora, Avila and Segovia were all easily secured by the army. Other successes came in Zaragoza, captured by General Miguel Cabanellas, and, crucially, Seville, secured by General Queipo de Llano in the face of considerable odds. The capture of this southern city was essential for the later transfer of the Army of Africa to the European mainland.

Colonel Antonio Aranda, who initially declared for the Republic, secured the Asturian city of Oviedo for the rebels once a column of armed miners had set off to collaborate in the defence of Madrid; a partial siege of the city would be maintained by the Republicans until late in 1937. Aranda's trickery added weight to the opinions of those in the Republican zone for whom no trust could be placed in the remnants of the old army. Finally, within two days, the north-western province of Galicia, with the cities of Vigo and La Coruña and the port of El Ferrol, also fell to the rebels.

As soon as the situation settled Franco's star began to rise. He was in command of 32,000 of Spain's best troops, whose professionalism and experience were badly needed on the mainland. Moreover, two potential rivals for power had been eliminated by their respective failures. General Fanjul, along with Falangists and some troops, launched the Madrid rising on 19 July, occupying the Montaña barracks in the hope of holding out until aid arrived from outside the capital. It did not, and they were lynched by a crowd which stormed the barracks the following day, incensed by what it viewed as the fraudulent use of a white flag. Fanjul, arrested, was later executed by the Republican government. Meanwhile, by the time General Manuel Goded arrived in Barcelona to take command of the rising in the Catalan capital, the troops he was to have led had already lost the initiative in the face of resistance from the police and, above all, the CNT. Anarcho-syndicalists had stormed arms deposits after Lluys Companys, president of the Generalitat, refused to distribute arms to civilians, adding their numbers and experience in urban warfare to the defence of the Republic. Had either of these two generals succeeded, their claims for leadership would have been difficult to dispute. On 20 July, moreover, the generals' appointed figurehead, Sanjurjo, died in a plane crash while leaving Portugal for Spain. Franco had only one rival left – Emilio Mola, the organizer of a failed coup, whom Franco, although a younger man, outranked. The vacuum left by Sanjurjo's death, however, was filled immediately, if nominally, by the most senior general among the rebels, Cabanellas, who became the head of a Junta de Defensa Nacional, formed on 23 July by the senior rebel commanders in order to hold power in a collective fashion. Despite these efforts, by 10 August Franco was being described as commander-in-chief of the rebel forces by *The Times*. Three days earlier Franco had established his headquarters in Seville, and soon afterwards Mola agreed to leave all international contacts for the acquisition of supplies to Franco, a situation which, as we shall see, was to give Franco ever greater power, for it had quickly become obvious that without foreign aid the rebels were doomed to defeat. His power within the rebellion was constantly growing, and on 15 August, when Franco unilaterally decided to adopt the monarchist flag, he did so without consulting the Junta de Defensa Nacional, which had not yet agreed to any political blueprint for the future of Spain. His action, which broke with Mola's pre-rising plans, met with no public response from the Junta.

As the Republic tore itself apart, the Nationalist camp, as it was increasingly referred to, dominated by military opinion, sought the safety and efficiency of a unified command. On 21 September the Junta, meeting in an air base near Salamanca in the presence of some other generals, took the decision to make Franco the army's commander-in-chief, or Generalísimo. Franco was the most obvious choice. Cabanellas and Queipo de Llano had both undistinguished service records and what could be considered, under the new circumstances, chequered political pasts, having been supporters of the Republic. Mola, who had organized the rising, was in part discredited by its failure. Franco was not, however, content with the power and duties of a military commander, always vulnerable to the changing tide of battle. His belief in his providential qualities and undoubted political ambitions, coupled with the extraordinary circumstances opened to him by others' failure, led Franco to unite military and political authority, placing himself securely at the heart of the discussions over the future course for Spain – something which the generals had not yet turned to in detail. On 28 September, the day after the relief of the besieged military academy of Toledo, Franco and three senior officers loyal to him – Luis Orgaz, Alfredo Kindelán and Juan Yagüe – returned to Salamanca to meet with the other generals and to propose that Franco assume the title of head of state for the duration of the conflict. A hysterical mob was on hand to cheer Franco in the aftermath of his military victory, while Yagüe insisted that his foreign legion, arguably the most efficient unit in the army, demanded Franco's elevation. It took a day's argument to reach a compromise, Franco accepting the title of head of government instead; but on his first public appearance Franco referred to himself as head of the Spanish state, a title immediately echoed by the press in the Nationalist zone. This was a coup within the coup, but one which the other generals did not feel sufficiently strong to challenge. The passing of the military Junta was underlined when Franco alone created a Junta Técnica – in all but name a government – charged with the task of running the country. This Junta Técnica was made up of seven executive commissions and was presided by General Fidel Dávila, who had no political ambitions of his own. The war would be fought according to Franco's orders and his vision would guide the creation of a new Spain.

CHAPTER THREE

The course of the war

A generalized civil war was not the intention of the military rebels in July 1936. Their goal was rather to capture power using great violence; but this was to be done in a sudden way, with the military authorities in complete control of the coup. Civilian support had been negotiated in order to make this task easier; however, it was clear to all that Carlists and the Falange would act in support of the military, adding to the impression of an irresistible force taking control of the country. The coup failed and the rebel officers were left in a difficult position. Compromise was impossible and a war had to be fought against a more numerous enemy which controlled two-thirds of the population, the country's main cities and its principal industrial areas, and which, forming as it did the internationally recognized government of Spain, should, in theory, find it easier to obtain whatever raw materials, weapons or ammunition might be needed in order to win the war. In this chapter we will examine how this situation was overcome by the military rebels and, conversely, how the Republic saw all of its trump cards bested.

The military history of the Spanish Civil War is one of frustration on both sides. The Republic never won a lasting victory in an offensive battle; all of its victories were defensive, the most notable being the Battle of Madrid late in 1936. Unfortunately for the Republic, even these defensive victories were not sufficiently decisive. Republican strongholds gradually fell to the Nationalist forces, whose greater cohesion and unity of purpose, as well as vital foreign supplies of weapons, allowed them to undo the shaky political and territorial coalition that faced them. First Andalusia and Extremadura, then the Basque Country and Asturias, and finally

Aragon and Catalonia: one by one the regions of Spain were isolated and captured by the forces loyal to Franco, who subsequently harnessed local resources to the Nationalist war effort in a way that the Republicans never matched.

There was, however, much frustration in the Nationalist camp, especially among Franco's foreign allies. After the failure of his bid to capture Madrid in 1936, Franco's strategy changed to a slow conquest of Spain, allowing for the steady identification and punishment of Republicans, socialists, communists and anarchists in the conquered areas. The war became a slow purge of Spanish society, despite the belief of many on Franco's side that the war could be won quickly if conducted in a more aggressive fashion.

3.1 THE DRIVE FOR MADRID

After their failure to seize power quickly, the rebels controlled only Galicia, Navarre, northern Castile and Leon, as well as the cities of Oviedo and Seville, the Moroccan protectorate, Majorca and the Canary Islands – hardly worthwhile springboards for concerted and swift action. Mola, who was supposed to advance on Madrid from Pamplona, the Navarrese capital, could only spare 5,000 men for that purpose, having to protect his flanks and seal up the Basque Country. Out of touch with each other, the rebel commanders could expect, in normal circumstances, to be defeated one by one. Supplies were an obvious weakness: Mola's forces came close to running out of ammunition, which led him to dispatch emissaries to Germany and Italy asking for supplies. These, however, were not normal times, because the rebels' action had triggered – although not in the way that they expected – the disintegration of the Republic, which could not bring its strength to bear on the various patches of rebel-controlled territory. In order to protect its existence, the Republic disbanded the remaining army units and distributed their weapons to party and union militias, but armed workers, lacking reliable military intelligence, military discipline and logistics, could not be expected to conquer territory in set-piece battles against experienced military and paramilitary formations. Successful, if limited, actions were possible only where the police was on the side of the militias. Few restraints kept militiamen in the front against their will and, in many cases, notably among the anarchist militias, troops were entitled to vote for or against the merit of orders passed down from above.

Of 12,000 or so officers in the Spanish army, 7,000 sided with the rebels, but of those in the Republican zone 1,500 were murdered, 1,500 were dismissed and 1,000 went into hiding. Very few professional officers were therefore allowed to contribute with their training to the Republic's defence. Mola and the other surviving rebel leaders were thus given time to breathe and consolidate their defences, despite supply difficulties and the government's control of the Spanish air force. The militias facing them, believing that victory would ultimately be theirs, were essentially content to defend territory, such as the mountain ranges to the north of Madrid, or to attack cities and fortresses which were already completely surrounded and whose continued resistance frustrated them, Oviedo and the Alcázar of Toledo being the clearest cases. This inescapably defensive posture, which would dominate the Republican war effort until 1937, but which was so crucial in the days following the defeat of the coup, allowed the more dynamic rebel commanders to come to the fore, none more so than Franco, and Germany and Italy to begin supplying the rebels with badly needed arms and munitions.

Franco benefited from his position as rebel commander in Morocco in many ways. With the situation in Spain locked into a stalemate, all eyes turned to him, especially those of his colleagues who, in an ever more difficult situation, considered his arrival on the Spanish mainland to be the only means to achieve victory. For the Republic, keeping Franco at bay was a priority, and for foreign observers he was the man capable of resolving a confused situation. From being relatively unknown to the rest of the world – 'brother of the well-known airman', *The Times* called him on 20 July, in a reference to Ramón Franco, who had flown across the Atlantic – Franco quickly became the main protagonist. The foreign legion and the Moroccan regulars, 32,000 of the most professional troops in the Spanish army, were now under Franco's direct command. If a significant proportion of these troops landed in Spain then the military situation would certainly change, with the rebels being able to break through from their isolated positions, finally regaining the strategic initiative. The transfer of the grandly titled Army of Africa to the mainland was to prove significant in a number of ways. Franco's forces allowed the transformation, on the rebels' side, of the coup into a war, improving Franco's claim to leadership in the wake of Sanjurjo's death. Until its arrival at the gates of Madrid, the Army of Africa proved to be an irresistible force. Finally, the need for aircraft to fly the Army of Africa to Spain led to the involvement of Germany and Italy on the rebels' side, a factor that would prove crucial to both Franco's rise within the Nationalist hierarchy and his eventual military victory. Before the arrival of German and Italian aircraft, Franco could only send 200 men per day to Seville by air.

The transfer of the Army of Africa to Europe was thus the first key challenge for Franco. Once again it seemed that the odds were stacked on the Republic's side. On paper, Spain's navy was overwhelmingly Republican. The government controlled the battleship *Jaime I*, three cruisers, ten destroyers and twelve submarines; the rebels, after the capture of El Ferrol, in Galicia, had one battleship, the *España*, two cruisers in dry dock, one destroyer, five small torpedo boats and two submarines; they also controlled the shipyards where two cruisers were being finished – the *Canarias* and the *Baleares*. However, a very substantial and bloody purge of officers carried out by sailors on the Republic's warships had left a toothless force in place. Those officers who survived were embittered and the military efficiency of the Republican navy was to remain low throughout the conflict. Nevertheless, what remained was sufficient to blockade the African coast, preventing Franco from bringing his men to Spain. Franco's answer was twofold: to fly in the troops, a lengthy and costly exercise which could only take place quickly with the aid of foreign powers, and to remove the Republican navy from the scene. Mussolini and Hitler, after days of hesitation, offered Franco the aeroplanes necessary to perform both tasks (while Britain refused access to Gibraltar to Republican warships, making their refuelling more difficult), and the foreign legion and the Moroccan troops began to be ferried to Seville, where they were assembled without interference from the forces loyal to the Republic. On 5 August, soon after the aerial transport of troops began, Franco, who now enjoyed aerial supremacy over the Straits of Gibraltar, risked a shipment of troops by sea. This operation went according to plan, ensuring the immediate success of the rebels' cause in the south.

Once in Spain with his army, Franco began to push northwards along the Portuguese border, which protected his left flank. The Portuguese government willingly provided a terrestrial link for the rebel forces in the south and north of Spain, one of the many favours that António Oliveira Salazar granted Franco during the Civil War. On the open ground of Extremadura, the Army of Africa proved too skilful for the disorganized and inexperienced militias that faced it.

Simple outflanking manoeuvres by Yagüe's troops repeatedly carried the day against the militias, whose morale plummeted as the number of defeats mounted; in one week the Army of Africa advanced 200 kilometres. By 10 August it had conquered Mérida, establishing tenuous contact with the rest of the rebel forces; in mid-August the important border town of Badajoz, defended by a garrison of 800 soldiers and 1,000 volunteers, fell to Yagüe's column, diverted to it by Franco's order. The number of Republicans shot in the town – up to 2,000 – and the systematic way in which the reprisals were carried out, provided Republican propaganda with its first set of atrocity stories and damaged the insurgent cause abroad. The Moroccan troops employed by Franco were especially singled out in Republican propaganda: not only were they foreigners, whose use in Spain was in breach of arrangements with the Sultan of Morocco, but they were accused of the savage treatment of prisoners and civilians, including women. Franco was not troubled by such arguments, and as many as 78,000 Moroccans would fight in the war on his side.

In the foreign press it quickly became apparent that the war had become a mismatch. Forces loyal to the Republic might be able to defend mountainous territory against Mola's inexperienced troops and Carlist volunteers, but they simply could not hold open ground against the Moroccans. It was now assumed that the war would not last until 1937, but that Franco would simply march into Madrid and topple the regime. Whether this would have been possible remains contentious; the truth is that Franco willingly directed his forces away from Madrid in order to relieve the siege of the Alcázar, in Toledo, whose importance in propaganda terms had become paramount. In the meantime, Portugal served as a supply route for ammunition to Mola, who was able to undertake offensive operations against the Basque Country; on 4 September he captured Irún, closing off the Basques' links to France, and on the 13th he took San Sebastián. Mola's northern actions effectively sealed the division of the Republic into two distinct territories, and cut off the bulk of its troops from the Basque Country's heavy industry, creating a logistical and economic nightmare.

We have already seen that the military rebels benefited from the unambiguous support of Portugal, Italy and Germany. The Republicans, however, were not to enjoy the benefits of foreign intervention to such a great extent. The Spanish Civil War coincided with the years of appeasement, when the Fascist regime in Rome and its Nazi counterpart in Berlin set about destroying the post-Versailles order, predicated upon the notion of collective security underwritten by the League of Nations. Although militarily stronger, France and Britain stood by and watched as Italy invaded Ethiopia, and Germany annexed both Austria and Czechoslovakia. The traumas left by the First World War dominated political life in the Western democracies which had triumphed in 1918, leaving them with no desire for a renewed confrontation with Germany. Although France's own Popular Front government, led by Léon Blum, was willing, for a brief period of time, to supply arms to a Spanish government which it saw as legitimate, British warnings about the need to prevent the spreading of the Spanish conflict and strident opposition from every point on the French political spectrum soon forced Blum to change course. While the sale of French arms was reined in, the presence of German and Italian arms and men was to play a significant part in Franco's military triumph.

The only country that came to the aid of the Republic in a consistent fashion – in so far as it was willing to sell it weapons, in return for the immediate transfer of Spain's gold reserves – was the Soviet Union. There was also some military aid from Mexico, but this was both irregular in arrival and essentially confined to ammunition. Having concluded a treaty with France in 1935, Stalin saw the war in Spain as a chance to reinforce that treaty, hopefully entangling Britain as well. Stalin believed that the Spanish Republic was under threat from internal fascists aided by Italy and Germany, and that this was a scenario that would wake France and Britain from their lethargy and force them to take the fascist threat seriously. If the Spanish Republic remained in existence and fighting for survival, thanks to Soviet arms, the battle lines between fascist and anti-fascist states would eventually be drawn. Stalin was disappointed in the end, changing course through a treaty of non-aggression with Germany in 1939, but for over two years Soviet weapons – artillery, tanks and aeroplanes, all capable of matching those in the Nationalists' expanding arsenal – and advisers arrived in Spain's eastern ports in sufficient numbers to prolong the conflict, preventing the sudden collapse of the Republican regime. In October 1936, coinciding with the first Soviet arms shipments, the first batch of men who would make up the International Brigades arrived in Spain, receiving their training in Albacete; a French communist, André Marty, was their authoritarian and controversial commander. Although not exclusively communist, the International Brigades had the Red Army as their model, with political commissars accompanying officers. All told, over 60,000 men would serve in the Brigades, 20,000 of whom were Spaniards. The International Brigades were deployed as shock troops in what, to the Republican government, were the war's most important battlefields – Madrid, Jarama, Guadalajara, Brunete, Teruel and the Ebro. Many came from Germany and Italy, countries to which they could not return until their present regimes had been defeated; others originated in the Western democracies, embarrassed by their governments' inaction: 10,000 from France, 2,800 from the United States and 2,000 from Britain. Their presence, numbers and dedication were to add considerably to the peculiar character of the Spanish Civil War. In the words of one historian, 'hindsight about the awful crimes of Stalin or about the sordid power struggles within the Republican zone cannot diminish the idealism and heroism of those who sacrificed their comfort, their security and often their lives in the anti-fascist struggle' (Preston 1996a: 126).

The fortress of the Alcázar in Toledo, home to the army's infantry academy, was to become another of the enduring symbols of the Civil War. Its defenders were mostly Civil Guards, with only a smattering of cadets present. Most of their colleagues were at home for the holidays. In the fortress there were also the families of the defenders and a number of hostages, whose presence would be blotted out in Nationalist accounts. In these accounts, the Alcázar was defended by the fine flower of Spanish youth, commanded by the indomitable General Moscardó, who, it was said, had sacrificed the life of his son rather than surrender the fortress to the Republican besiegers. Much of the Alcázar's importance was derived from the energy with which the workers' militias attacked it (in part a consequence of the taking of hostages). Toledo's proximity to Madrid also made it a favourite target for the militiamen who returned to Madrid after a day's sniping. Even cabinet ministers went to Toledo to see how the attack was proceeding. The Alcázar, however, was of little military value, and the forces loyal to the Republic should have concentrated their efforts on halting the arrival in Spain of the Army of Africa. The same criticism could be directed at the Nationalists, who would have been wiser to attempt to capture Madrid, after which the siege would automatically be lifted. For Franco, however, the relief of the Alcázar would be a different victory from that, for example, of

Badajoz. It would show the world that Franco was a general whose sense of honour was greater than his desire for a quick victory, a chivalrous man who was capable of defeating his enemies where and when he wanted. Foreign opinion, trying to make sense of events in Spain, had mistakenly latched on to the Alcázar as an example of bravery and heroism, ignoring the presence of hostages and concentrating on the virtue displayed by the mostly absent cadets. *The Times*, on 1 October 1936, called it 'the one relieving feature of the whole miserable struggle'. The greatest impact of the relief of the Alcázar was on Franco's bid for complete political and military control of the Nationalist cause, and his triumphal entry into the fortress late in September was repeated the day after it originally took place for the benefit of the cameras.

3.2 FIGHTING IN AND AROUND MADRID

After the capture of Toledo, Franco once again pointed his armies in the direction of Madrid. Whether success at the Alcázar compromised his army's ability to take the capital quickly cannot established, but, without a doubt, the pause that ensued was of benefit to the defenders. In the capital, deserted by the government which had left for the safety of the coastal city of Valencia (Prime Minister Francisco Largo Caballero being sure that the city would fall), the PCE took it upon itself to make a stand, rallying the city's population for defence. The successful effort to hold Madrid, which defied all predictions, was without a doubt the high point of the Republic's war effort and, along with the failure of the July coup, determined the course of the war until 1939. Franco's reluctance to attack Madrid again after his initial failure ensured that there could be no quick solution to the conflict. Madrid was governed, after the departure of the cabinet, by a Popular Front Junta presided over by General José Miaja and defended by militias whose morale was boosted by a number of factors: intelligent and persistent propaganda activity; the perspective of fighting not on open ground but in a city, the battlefield of the many revolutions in Spain's recent past; the arrival of Soviet weapons (notably fighter planes, which regained control of the skies over the capital, and tanks, which participated in a local counter-attack on 29 October); and the arrival of the International Brigades. The capture of the Nationalist battle plan helped the defenders to allocate their resources effectively. For three weeks in November 1936, with Mola,

Varela and Yagüe commanding the attacking troops, fighting raged in Madrid's western suburbs, in parks, and in the new University City. So confident of victory were the Nationalist commanders that they were willing to attack a large city with only 20,000 men at their disposal. For the first time, although at tremendous cost, the Republic's forces (whose number, difficult to estimate, included over 20,000 militiamen reinforced by the International Brigades and the 1,500 anarchists brought by the charismatic anarchist leader Buenaventura Durrutti) held against the Army of Africa. On 22 November the Nationalist assault was called off, and the rebel generals, stunned by their defeat, feared the worst should a Republican counter-attack be launched. Madrid was saved, and with victory came a new prestige for the PCE: it had remained in place, refusing to believe victory impossible; its international contacts – not the government's – had brought weapons of the highest quality; and brave and determined communists from all over the world had come to fight Franco's Moroccans.

On 20 November 1936 Durrutti died in confused circumstances in Madrid, where he had led his column in an effort to support the defence of the city; but his efforts were not sufficient to dispel the doubts raised by the PCE over the lack of Catalan and anarchist support for the embattled capital. It has taken recent research into the anarchists' contribution to the war effort to dispel this impression. Durrutti's funeral in Barcelona, attended by hundreds of thousands of mourners, was an impressive demonstration of his popularity with anarchists, and of the CNT's strength in the Catalan capital. It could do nothing, however, to overturn the political prestige accumulated by the communists that month.

The attack on Madrid also provided the world with a picture which had so far been the preserve of science fiction – the attempted destruction of a capital city by modern bombers. This aerial campaign was followed with close attention by military authorities everywhere. A delegation of British MPs was told, late in November, that 365 people had already been killed in the raids, and that nearly 2,000 had been wounded; during their stay in the Spanish capital the British parliamentarians witnessed an air raid, which moved them to write to Franco, protesting against the deliberate targeting of civilian areas, which they termed an 'outrage'. Waves of aeroplanes were sent against the city, where life became increasingly difficult: hundreds of thousands of refugees had entered it before the arrival of Franco's army, and the arrival of foodstuffs became less frequent as the fighting worsened. The quality of bread, still available plentifully, deteriorated considerably. Militia units received priority in the allocation of resources; union members could rely on their connections and union cards to feed themselves; the rest, especially the refugees, suffered most. Nevertheless, morale in the city held, revealing the limitations of aerial terror campaigns that would be confirmed in the Second World War.

His frontal attack on Madrid having failed, Franco decided to change tactics, attempting to isolate Madrid from the rest of Republican-held territory. In order to bring this about Franco ordered an attack along the Jarama River, and, when this failed, gave the Italian units fighting alongside his army the green light for a lightning attack – whose virtues were proclaimed by the Italians – in Guadalajara, in order to cut the Valencia road. The Italians, whose arrival in large numbers in the port of Cadiz had been well documented by the international press, had already contributed to the fall of Malaga on 8 February 1937. Malaga's police force had declared for the Republic in July 1936, thus foiling the plan of the rebel officers stationed in the city. Malaga had been almost completely isolated from the rest of Republican territory since the start of the war, and had been the stage for some of the most brutal executions of suspected Nationalist sympathizers – although these massacres took place only after a series of bombing raids on the town by the Nationalist air force late in July 1936. According to a British eye-witness, P. Chalmers Mitchell, writing to *The Times* on 20 October 1936, the bombs were dropped from a great height, from which accuracy was impossible, with the result that civilian areas were badly hit – after which violence broke out against officers and other supposed supporters of Franco. Eventually, Malaga was easily taken by a joint Spanish–Italian force, and much of its population fled by road to Almeria, being shelled from naval vessels and strafed from the air along the way – another horrific foreshadowing of events in the Second World War which did much to hurt the Nationalist cause in foreign eyes. After the fall of Malaga to the Nationalists the most violent reprisals so far in the war were carried out, up to 4,000 people being killed in one week.

The failure of the frontal attack on Madrid, meanwhile, allowed the Republican government to reinforce further its defences. Largo Caballero, prime minister and leader of the PSOE and the UGT, had the authority needed to amalgamate militia units and begin to build a homogeneous Republican army. Madrid, as a result, continued to hold out, the encircling attempts in the Jarama Valley failing despite high casualties on both sides (up to 10,000 for the Republicans, and up to 6,000 for the attacking Nationalists, a proportion which reveals the gap in efficiency between the two armies). After their victory in the south, the Italian units were rushed to the line, attacking in light tropical uniforms despite the winter conditions, which also prevented Nationalists from enjoying air superiority. After initial gains, the Italian attack, launched on 8 March and comprising over 30,000 men – regular soldiers and Fascist Party blackshirts – stalled and turned into a rout. The Italians blamed Franco for the defeat. A Spanish attack, to have been led by the hero of the Alcázar, Moscardó, had barely moved, allowing Republicans to concentrate their forces, including Soviet tanks and, ironically, Italian International Brigaders, against the Italian expeditionary force. Franco was not completely displeased by the outcome, which had dented Italian arrogance and self-belief while tying Mussolini more closely to the Nationalist cause: Mussolini declared that Italian forces would remain on the field until they had avenged the defeat of Guadalajara. Nearly 1,000 Italians died in the disaster, with another 2,500 being wounded and 800 captured.

3.3 THE NORTHERN CAMPAIGN

On the whole, the winter of 1936–7 was a success for the Republic, whose military had grown stronger with the arrival of Soviet weapons, the International Brigades and, most importantly, the creation of the new Popular Army to replace the obviously inefficient militias. The Popular Army was a regular military force with an officer corps seconded by political commissars, and was designed to match the Nationalists' fighting power while sponsoring a high level of political awareness and attachment to the Republic's cause among its troops. Despite its creation, however, the successes of that winter were to be the last for the Republic; after them a long and inexorable series of defeats would follow. May 1937 especially marked a low point in the Republic's history. While the May Days raged in Barcelona (see Chapter 4), the Largo Caballero government collapsed, and a series of purges and internal territorial struggles broke out in Republican territory, Franco's forces were sent against first the Basque Country and then into Asturias. Their success demonstrated once again the advantages of a unified political and military command structure. With Madrid to their south, Asturias to their northwest and Aragon to their east, the Nationalists nevertheless turned north with near impunity, overrunning the Basque Country without having their flanks consistently harried.

The Basque campaign of 1937 was a notable success in military terms for Franco, who, despite the fierce resistance that was met, the poor weather and the death of the local commander, General Mola, in a plane crash on 3 June 1937, was able to seize and exploit the region's industrial might. The campaign was also notable because of the controversial use of air power to hurry the collapse of the Basques' will to resist. The towns of Durango and Guernica were razed to the ground in raids which in 1937 were a novelty that greatly impressed public opinion. The Guernica raid was especially heavy, the bombardment lasting for hours and being punctuated by the strafing of civilians by fighter planes. The plight of Guernica, the town in which Spanish monarchs had traditionally sworn to respect Basque laws, the *fueros*, and whose suffering was immortalized by Picasso, symbolized the advent of a new dawn in warfare, a time in which war became total, civilians being considered as legitimate a target as soldiers. The fact was sufficiently shocking at the time (*The Times*, on 28 April 1937, described events in Guernica as 'the pitiless bombardment of a country town, the centre of Basque tradition and culture, by an air fleet which encountered no resistance and did practically no damage to the scanty military objectives beneath it') to force the Nationalists to invent and propagate – not without success in conservative circles abroad – their own version of events in the ancient Basque town. According to this tale, Guernica had been burnt by the retreating forces as part of a scorched-earth policy. A communiqué sent to the foreign press from the Nationalist headquarters in Salamanca stressed the scale of 'Red atrocities', which included air raids on hospitals, before going on to argue that Guernica, as a staging area and a centre for the manufacture of weapons, was indeed a legitimate target, and to deny that the Nationalist air force had been responsible for the town's destruction – a clear case of propaganda overkill.

Air superiority was indeed the key to Franco's Basque victory. It was conferred by the German Condor Legion, whose newest machines were superior to Soviet fighters which, in any case, were not present in sufficient numbers in the sector. Some accounts mention the way in which German bombers circled lazily over Bilbao, displaying their invulnerability to the people below. As had happened in the case of Madrid, the population of Bilbao was swollen with over 100,000 refugees who were fed only with the greatest of difficulties, eyewitnesses speaking of a famine in the city in the weeks prior to its fall. International agencies were able to remove 14,000 children from the Basque Country (and 1,200 from Asturias), who were then sent to Britain, France and the USSR. Bilbao's system of fortified defences, the supposedly impregnable 'ring of iron', was not finished by the time it was stormed on 12 June (and in any case the Nationalist commanders had received plans showing the disposition of the existing emplacements). Thirty thousand Basque soldiers, inexperienced and previously ordered to hold their borders rather than to come to the defence of Madrid, found it impossible to resist the onslaught of 50,000 Nationalists, in which the Navarrese brigades, composed of the Carlist militia, had pride of place. Nationalist troops found their way through a half-mile gap in the defences, and the population of Bilbao did not demonstrate Madrid's fighting spirit: not even the factories coveted by Franco were destroyed when the city fell on 19 June 1937. After the fall of Bilbao would come the fall of Santander (also swollen with refugees, thousands of whom were removed by ship) on 24 August. The capture of Santander by Italian troops was the 'revenge' so badly sought by Mussolini who, nevertheless, could not bring himself to withdraw his forces from the Spanish conflict. The fall of the city resulted in the capture of 60,000 prisoners – the single largest surrender of the war. Manuel Azaña was informed that the Nationalist troops had cut through the Basque Country as quickly as if they had been on a simple exercise: after the loss of their capital, the Basques' will to fight had simply evaporated (Azaña 1990: 846).

The end of the fighting on the northern front came with the fall of Asturias, which was delayed until October 1937 thanks to stiff resistance in the face of overwhelming odds and occasional Republican attacks in other sectors. On 6 July the Republic launched its first major attack, near Madrid, towards the town of Brunete. Under the overall command of a new chief of staff, Vicente Rojo, this was intended as a showcase battle for the Popular Army. Five out of the six divisions employed were commanded by communists; the communist-organized Fifth Corps was there, as were the International Brigades, used, as ever, as shock troops. In the terrible

Castilian summer heat, 59,000 men went forward, aided by 128 tanks, but were stopped after only one week as Franco switched troops and aeroplanes from the north, launching a counter-attack that by 25 July had recovered Brunete. At that stage Franco called the operation to a halt against the advice of General José Varela, who believed – not without reason, considering the state of the Republican forces – that Madrid could be taken. One fact became clear at Brunete: the Republic's lack of experienced officers made it difficult to coordinate offensive action, which meant that unforeseen circumstances on the battlefield quickly led to paralysis. Equally ominous were the reports which reached Azaña about desertion during the attack: half of the 20,000 Republican casualties had been caused by soldiers surreptitiously heading home (Azaña 1990: 756). Another Republican offensive was launched in August, in Aragon, towards the city of Zaragoza; once again, however, 80,000 Republicans, including the rested Fifth Corps and the International Brigades, and 100 tanks, were halted by the Nationalists, thanks in part to the determined defence by Falangist and Carlist troops of the town of Belchite. The eventual capture by the Nationalists of Asturias brought with it the end of the longest siege of the war, that of Oviedo, defended for over a year since the revolt by Colonel Aranda and the garrison loyal to him. With the Asturian government fleeing, and Republican policemen deserting to the Nationalist forces, the Republican besiegers surrendered to the Nationalist besieged.

3.4 THE FINAL CAMPAIGNS

With the fall of the Basque Country and of Asturias, the strategic situation of the Republic's government became far more precarious. It was confined to the eastern half of Spain, having lost access to the Atlantic; this being the case, its sole remaining coastline could be easily blockaded by the increasingly powerful Nationalist navy and air force, seconded in this task by not inconsiderable Italian detachments. Republican casualties had been high in the northern campaign, with 33,000 killed, 100,000 taken prisoner and 100,000 wounded. The Republic had lost 1.5 million citizens, 36 per cent of its industrial output, 60 per cent of its coal production and almost all of its steel production. Finally, the distance that separated Nationalist forces from the Mediterranean Sea was slight, and should that small corridor of land be captured then Catalonia would be cut off from the rest of the Republic. Not surprisingly it was here that the Nationalists struck next, after having switched 65,000 soldiers from the north to the east.

Naval warfare in 1937 was of extreme importance. Control of the sea was essential for the survival of the Republic because weapons, ammunition and vital foodstuffs could only arrive by ship, due to France's closure of the border with Spain. The cutting off of the maritime supply route was a priority for Franco. That summer the sinking of merchant ships in the western Mediterranean became a common occurrence, and even patrolling foreign warships were attacked in actions described by the international press as piracy. One of the most significant events of this naval war was the severe damage caused by Republican aeroplanes to the German battleship *Deutschland* as she lay at anchor in Ibiza on 26 May. According to Azaña, the attacking pilots were Russian, and they had mistaken the German ship for the *Canarias*. Thirty-one sailors were killed and in retaliation another German warship, the cruiser *Admiral Scheer*, shelled the town of Almeria with impunity. In June the German navy would claim that another cruiser, the *Leipzig*, had twice been attacked near Oran, a charge that was never proved. In retaliation, Germany and Italy withdrew its ships from the naval patrol supposedly enforcing non-intervention, while Portugal ordered the end of international control over its border with Spain. The majority of attacks in the Mediterranean was carried out by Nationalist and Italian submarines. In August 1937 Franco's brother Nicolás was in Rome asking for more of these vessels, a request to which Mussolini agreed. Mallorca was used as a base by Italian submarines flying a Spanish flag. By September, as the attacks increased, the British government decided to strengthen its presence in the area. Once again, though, mounting tension was defused by an inconclusive international assembly. That very month a conference took place in Nyon, in Switzerland, to allocate patrol areas in the Mediterranean in order to bring the sinkings to a halt. Italy, widely suspected of being responsible for the attacks, withdrew from the talks, along with Germany, after a row with the USSR. On 14 September Britain and France agreed on the division of the western Mediterranean into patrol zones. Mussolini's subsequent complaints over Italy's exclusion from the patrols saw a revision of the accords on the 27 September by which the Italian navy, whose ships were largely responsible for the attacks, received its own patrol zone. This was an unequivocal demonstration of the absurdity of non-intervention, which had little to do with Spain and everything with mediating conflicts between Europe's stronger countries at the Republic's expense.

The Nationalist drive to the sea was precipitated by the third great Republican offensive, the initially successful bid to capture Teruel and its population of 20,000, launched in December 1937, after a period of rest and reorganization for both sides. In November 1937, the Nationalist army stood at 600,000 men, while the Popular Army's total strength was 450,000 men. Despite this imbalance, the Republican High Command believed that a successful offensive operation might turn the war around. By Christmas Teruel had been stormed, despite last-ditch resistance by Colonel Rey d'Harcourt, the Nationalist commander, which continued until 8 January (the units under his orders suffered a 75 per cent casualty rate, a demonstration of the high morale among the Nationalists). International praise for the Republican army's success was fulsome. *The Times*, describing it as a 'well planned and cleanly won victory', called Teruel 'the greatest achievement of the republican new army'. The Republican forces did not, however, achieve a breakthrough after the capture of this provincial capital, and Nationalist reinforcements were rushed from all over Spain to Aragon until their numbers overwhelmed the Republicans facing them. The Nationalist offensive, which achieved a breakthrough on 18 January 1938, proved unstoppable, despite the atrocious winter conditions in which the fighting took place: the imbalance of the forces in the field and in the air became obvious as the Republican front slowly crumbled. Teruel fell to the Nationalists a month later, with thousands of prisoners being taken, and what followed was a succession of offensives that allowed Nationalists to reach the Mediterranean on 15 April 1938. The war had become an undignified rout, in which Nationalist forces had crossed the Ebro River and driven into Catalonia for the first time, capturing Lérida on 3 April despite resistance by the noted communist commander El Campesino. The capture of hydroelectric plants on 8 April cut a significant part of Barcelona's electricity supplies, affecting industrial production and the quality of life in the city. Although the front was eventually stabilized, thanks to the arrival of new weapons via France (Léon Blum, exasperated by the Anschluss, ordered the opening up of the border in order to allow armaments, including 300 Soviet aeroplanes, to pass through undisturbed), an impressive campaign of popular mobilization, repression of all 'defeatists', and desperate battles to protect the approaches to Valencia, there could be no doubt as to the ultimate winner of the Civil War. Teruel was of great importance to Franco. The Republican army had been beaten in a field of battle of its own choosing, and a difficult one at that, with high mountain ranges and low temperatures hampering the movement of troops. Nevertheless, Franco came under criticism from foreign experts once again: having reached the sea he had split his efforts, making an eventually unsuccessful bid to reach Valencia, when Barcelona, defenceless, had been his for the taking. By allowing Catalonia to recover, Franco left his northern flank vulnerable to the Republic's forces, reinvigorated by the newly arrived weaponry.

As the tide of war turned decisively against the Republic, international opinion began to focus as never before on the plight of refugees and civilians caught in the fighting. Franco did not intervene at any stage to halt aerial attacks on Republican cities, notably the eastern ports of Valencia, Alicante and Barcelona. This last city was subjected for the whole of 1938 to regular bombing which, combined with the increasing shortage of supplies and poor news from the front, finally paid off in terms of damaged morale. During the rush to the sea the attacks on the Catalan capital became especially violent. In one week in March, according to the correspondent of *The Times*, over 800 people were killed and 2,200 were injured in what had been the worst sustained bombing campaign of the war. These attacks were ordered directly by Mussolini, who did not bother to consult Franco. Foreign governments and charity organizations pleaded for a halt to these attacks, but their requests were brushed aside. Franco's propaganda machine, despite the Generalísimo's anger over Mussolini's actions, continued to defend the bombings, arguing that the cities were important military centres and therefore legitimate targets – and that civilian casualties resulted from the Republican insistence on housing non-combatants near military targets.

Amazingly, the conflict would drag on for nearly another year thanks in part to Franco's failure to reach Barcelona. Republican Prime Minister Juan Negrín saw the deterioration of the diplomatic situation in Europe as evidence of a coming generalized war between the Western democracies and the dictatorships of Germany and Italy that might spell salvation for the Republic. It was imperative to hold on, and occasionally the Republic's forces achieved successes; on 6 March 1938, for example, the cruiser *Baleares* was sunk by Republican warships with 726 officers and men killed. In his expectation of a European war Negrín was not wrong, but he underestimated the extent to which the governments of Britain and France were willing to appease those of Germany and Italy. At first Negrín pinned his hopes on the consequences of the Anschluss, and then on the Sudeten crisis. A European war still did not break out, however, and Negrín's government did not survive until the invasion of Poland, which finally precipitated the predicted conflict.

The desire to fight on was not unquestioned in the Republican quarter, where the voices calling out for a negotiated solution were increasing; many were those who had given up all hope of a clear military victory. Franco, however, through his cautious tactics, did not take advantage of this growing mood in the Republican zone, despite the exasperation that this approach to the war provoked in many quarters, especially in Rome, which wanted to disentangle itself from Spain.

The last throw of the dice by the Popular Army took place in 1938. The Ebro battle, longest and costliest of the whole war, was launched on 25 July. The Army of Catalonia crossed the river Ebro in the hope of cutting deep into the Nationalist pocket that separated Catalonia from the rest of Republican Spain. Their aim was to attack the bulk of the Nationalist forces from the rear, preventing them from reaching Valencia and enveloping Madrid. Not for the first time, the Republican military leadership achieved total surprise, forcing its Nationalist counterpart to abandon its immediate plans in order to adopt a defensive stance elsewhere. The offensive involved 80,000 Republican soldiers, supported by the new Soviet fighters and eighty artillery batteries. Command positions were, as usual, entrusted to communist officers, with Juan Modesto in overall charge of the battle and Enrique Líster commanding the elite Fifth Corps. Once again, however, initial success, applauded abroad, turned into a long and expensive stalemate as Franco ordered troops from quiet sectors to reinforce the Ebro front. The battle became one of attrition that the Republicans simply could not win. Outnumbered, outgunned and having lost control of the air, the Republican pockets to the south of the Ebro and the bridges and crossings which kept them in touch with Catalonia were mercilessly pounded for months until the Republicans were forced, in mid-November, to retreat back across the river. All this time air raids on Barcelona and Valencia continued in an attempt to terrorize the civilian population and prevent the arrival of food and military supplies. Franco, sure of eventual victory, moved slowly, choosing to employ artillery and aerial attacks to weaken defences; despite their material superiority, the Nationalists suffered 57,000 losses to the Republicans' 70,000. These numbers bear witness to the intensity of the fighting on the Ebro front. As had already happened after Teruel, retreat turned into a rout that was to last for the rest of the year, until the Nationalist forces arrived at the French border. Tarragona fell on 15 January 1939, and despite the reopening of the French border to allow the passage of arms into Spain, Barcelona fell almost without a fight on 26 January. Thoughts of resistance had been overwhelmed by the desire to escape and, like Bilbao, Barcelona disappointed those who had hoped for a second epic siege to prolong the war and save the Republic. The Army of Catalonia fought a retreating battle, but civilians did not rush to aid it. There was no will in the Catalan capital, after the May Days, constant military defeat, over one year of aerial bombardment and a bitter power struggle between the government and the Generalitat, to replicate the stand made by the citizens of Madrid. Hundreds of thousands of refugees, many of whom had already streamed into Barcelona, now sought refuge across the Pyrenees. With Britain and the USSR refusing to accept refugees, many would still be in French camps when the Second World War came. Those who stayed behind witnessed the fall of Barcelona and the return of indiscriminate murder to the city as the Falange killed with impunity.

The fall of Barcelona precipitated the last act of the Civil War. Negrín, back in Spain after fleeing to France, insisted on the need to fight and to resist until a European war broke out. Franco, despite British and French approaches, would not hear of a mediated settlement: for him only unconditional surrender was acceptable. The Republicans still had 400,000 men under arms in the central area, under General Miaja's command, but few now agreed with the prime minister about the need to fight on. The feeling abroad was that any further resistance was futile, and in late February an increasing number of foreign governments, including the British and French executives, recognized Franco's as the legitimate government of Spain. Prime Minister Neville Chamberlain, in the Commons, stated that any further resistance in Spain would only result in suffering and loss of life without altering the eventual outcome. The policy of resistance was by now restricted to the communists and their closest allies within the PSOE (despite the hostility to Negrín of both Largo Caballero and Prieto). These forces were isolated further still from the majority of public opinion when Azaña, in France, resigned from the presidency. Azaña had been informed by military authorities, in Negrín's presence, that the war could not now be won. Moreover, French and British recognition of Franco left him without an international role to play, while Spanish political life had imploded with the fall of Barcelona, leaving him with no internal role to play either.

The Republican war effort descended into a tragic farce on 5 March 1939 when Negrín's government was overthrown by a National Council of Defence led by Colonel Casado, commander of the Army of the Centre. The hero of Madrid, General Miaja, and the pacifist socialist Julian Besteiro were also part of this Republican coup, which had the support of anarchist officers. The day before, a confused rising in the port of Cartagena had preceded the defection of the Republican navy, which sought refuge in French North Africa. Casado, troubled by a series of military promotions decreed by Negrín that seemed to favour the communists, was sure that he could negotiate with Franco once the communists and their allies had been driven from power. He had made his doubts about continued resistance known to Negrín in February to no avail. In truth, though, even Negrín realized the impossibility of victory, urging his friends to prepare escape plans from Republican territory. Fierce resistance was put up against Casado in Madrid by communist units for over a week (three out of the four army corps in the area were commanded by communists), despite the lack of orders from the PCE's leadership, but this was eventually overcome. As the government fled abroad for a second time, accompanied by other leading figures of the Republican war effort, the National Council of Defence turned its attention to a negotiated settlement with the Nationalists, the real reason for its existence. Casado and his followers hoped that the sight of their troops fighting communists in Madrid would make Franco more amenable to a negotiated settlement that might guarantee the safety of Republican sympathizers. This was a vain hope. Not having negotiated when the situation was difficult, or even bleak, Franco could see no reason why he should negotiate when he had Madrid at his mercy. Franco's desired 'National Revolution' could only be built upon the complete defeat of all pro-Republic factions. The capital was especially vulnerable after a week of internal fighting had left 230 killed, 560 wounded and supplies at an all-time low.

The final attack began on 26 March, and two days later the city's surrender was agreed upon. Monarchist flags and fascist salutes from conservatives and opportunists greeted the Nationalist army as it paraded through the capital. In the end, all the tension between Negrín and the defenders of mediation – men like Azaña, Prieto and Casado – proved pointless, since mediation with Franco was always out of the question; the only possible argument was between resistance and total surrender.

Little opposition was put up against Franco's final push for the other areas in Republican hands: the Republic was dead and Republicans now cared only about their salvation abroad. The fleet's desertion stranded thousands of soldiers in coastal cities; instead of departing for the safety of exile they were left to face arrest and in many cases execution. On 1 April Franco called an end to the conflict. The fighting had cost the lives of 70,000 Nationalist soldiers, and of 125,000 defenders of the Republic; the wounded on both sides ran into hundreds of thousands.

CHAPTER FOUR

The Republicans' war

The question of whether authoritarian states wage war more successfully than democracies has long been a source of argument for historians. At first glance the experience of the Spanish Civil War might suggest that advantage lies with the authoritarian state's speed in decision making and the execution of orders. However, Republican Spain during the Civil War should not be compared to France, Britain and the USA in the world wars, because so much of the Republican government's effort was aimed at re-establishing its authority and legitimacy in the face of the popular revolution which greeted the military rising. Moreover, in order to accomplish this difficult task and fight a war, the Republic had to stretch the concept of democracy to its furthest limits, concentrating power in the executive branch: a badly depleted Cortes, devoid of conservative and moderate deputies, met only occasionally to sanction all of the government's decisions. The anarchists attempted to carry out their libertarian communist revolution in rural and urban areas, collectivizing land and the means of production, and to fight a revolutionary, rather than a conventional, war, which included the recourse to terror as a weapon. Actions such as these prevented the Republican government from assuming, from the start, the leadership of the war against the rebellious army, and were to earn the Republic much bad publicity abroad. The remaining factions and parties within the Republican camp, in order both to curb this revolution and create a more disciplined military machine, attempted, successfully, to recreate the Popular Front in wartime. The role of the Communist Party is particularly important in this regard. The communists were at the forefront of the attempt to re-establish the Republic's legal control over the whole of the territory controlled by its military forces. The communists also served as a link to the USSR, the sole foreign power to supply the Republican war machine in any significant form, which necessarily strengthened their hand within the Popular Front coalition.

4.1 THE REPUBLIC'S WARTIME LEADERS

The Spanish Republic barely survived the military coup of 18 July 1936. It did so in a very feeble position, not least because the army had played, up to the date of the rising, an important role in deterring revolutionary action. Most anarchists, whose principal organization, the CNT, lacked a centralized command structure, had viewed the Republic with extreme distrust since 1931. The material conditions of the CNT's membership had not improved significantly with the coming of the Republic, and the state had continued to be identified as the ultimate source of oppression. Individual anarchists continued to feel duty-bound to rise against the state whenever possible. Without the strength of the army and of most of the members of the various police forces to prop up the state, power fell to the street. The first response of the Spanish government to the coup was to seek an accommodation with the rebels. This was attempted by Diego Martínez Barrio, whose deliberately moderate government lasted less than twenty-four hours. Negotiations having failed, however, there was no recourse but to arm the people organized in union and party militias, the decision being taken by the incoming prime minister, José Giral. This meant arming many who had long sworn to destroy all vestiges of the state, whatever its current guise. In other words, the government, by arming the militias, armed many of its most intransigent enemies, who used this opportunity to further their aims. For the CNT and FAI militiamen, who in Barcelona had to seize arms, the Generalitat having refused initially to arm the people, the opportunities to rebuild society along libertarian lines opened up by this set of circumstances could not be wasted. In the immediate aftermath of the rising the rebels did not seem, at least in Barcelona, to pose too great a threat. In the Republican zone, therefore, the war became a tale of a complete breakdown of authority and the subsequent attempt to rebuild it – a process which had many pitfalls.

Four men would serve as Republican prime ministers during the Civil War, each lasting longer in office than his predecessor. Each prime minister symbolized a different approach to dealing with the rebellion. The first, Martínez Barrio, lasted less than a day in office despite the support of Manuel Azaña, having represented an attempt to reach a compromise with the rebel officers which sought to bring Mola into the government. Martínez Barrio's war minister was General Miaja, who, being loyal to the Republic but also a member of the UME, was seen as an ideal go-between. The intransigence of both rebel officers and working-class associations and parties put paid to that moderate approach and, with it, Martínez Barrio's putative government, making civil war inevitable. Francisco Largo Caballero, for example, threatened to unleash a social revolution if Martínez Barrio was not removed. He was duly replaced by José Giral Pereira, a chemistry professor, leading another exclusively republican cabinet that, nevertheless, had the support of Indalecio Prieto, who was to remain in close contact with Giral. This government was marked by the ultimately failed attempt to suppress the rebellion while restricting political power to republican politicians. This was impossible because, as a republican, Giral's voice carried no weight with the newly armed militias, and he was to prove powerless both to halt the violence of the first days of the war and to prevent the subversion of the regime's political institutions by revolutionary committees and militias. Giral was also unable to attract foreign support for the embattled regime, and was replaced in September by Largo Caballero. Nevertheless, Giral was able to lay down some important markers for the future of the Republic and its struggle to survive. In the last days of July, his government called to the colours two classes of reservists, a measure which went largely ignored. It then decreed the creation of a volunteer army, a measure in which it was supported enthusiastically, but exclusively, by the PCE, which immediately began to prepare its own military unit, initially known as the Fifth Regiment. Lastly, Giral oversaw the transformation of the loyal remains of the *Guardia Civil* into a new paramilitary organization, the Republican National Guard.

The appointment in September 1936 of the historic leader of Spanish socialism, Francisco Largo Caballero, as prime minister was of great importance. It marked the return of the Popular Front, an experiment which, it was hoped, would allow the greatest possible number of Spaniards to flock to the defence of the Republic from both Nationalists and internal uncontrollable elements. Coming as they did from the best-known leader of Spain's workers, and not from a bourgeois republican, Largo's appeals for the creation of a unified command did not fall on deaf ears; the state's authority began its *de facto* recovery under his stewardship. Largo Caballero's long political career had resulted in many enmities: with Prieto and his followers, with Azaña and with the CNT, which had long despised him for his collaboration with Primo de Rivera during the dictatorship. For the moment these conflicts were ignored. Prieto served loyally in the cabinet as air force and navy minister, realizing that only Largo Caballero would be able to work with the powerful CNT. Azaña learnt to live with Largo, for there was no option but to come to a mutual understanding. Even the CNT, in a dramatic move, agreed to enter the government, four of its moderate figures serving as ministers under Largo, including Federica Montseny, who became Spain's first female cabinet minister. As a prime minister, however, Largo quickly developed a new enemy, this time the increasingly assertive PCE. This was a surprising development, as prior to the war Largo Caballero and the communists had been growing closer, and as the communists had supported his nomination to the premiership. Largo was, however, a party and union man, and, like other socialists, was deeply protective of the organizations he had built up and now headed. He feared for the PSOE if it merged with the PCE, disliked the growing communist influence within the UGT, and resented both communist power within the new army (for which, as war minister, he was directly responsible) and the clear growth of Soviet influence in Spain. By the spring of 1937 the communists, disenchanted, were thinking of ways to remove Largo from his position.

The fourth and longest-serving prime minister of the war was Juan Negrín, aged forty-eight in 1937, a socialist academic and medical doctor who served as finance minister under Largo Caballero. During this time the efficient and energetic Negrín successfully carried out negotiations with the USSR for the supply of arms in return for Spain's gold reserves. Negrín, associated with Prieto's wing of the party, had had a secondary political role within the PSOE before the war, but he was an extraordinary man who would lead the Republic for nearly two years of constant military defeats and international isolation without relinquishing power. Under his leadership the Republic's assertion of its authority would reach its peak, while the newly created Popular Army would increase sufficiently in strength to launch major offensives such as those of Teruel and the Ebro. Negrín was publicly committed to all-out resistance against the Nationalist forces, arguing that compromise with them had become impossible and that Europe was headed for a general war in which Franco's fascist links would place him alongside Italy and Germany. In such a conflict the Republic would naturally gravitate to the side of France and Britain, both of which would then come to its rescue. Thus, all the Republic had to do was to hold tight and wait for Europe to go to war. What Negrín did not predict, however, was how much would be needed to prod Britain and France to go to war (the Anschluss and the invasion of Czechoslovakia not being enough), as well as Franco's clever diplomatic stance during the Austrian and Czechoslovak crises. Nationalist propaganda during these months stressed both Franco's neutrality in European affairs and his desire for good future relations with France and Britain. In the face of these setbacks, Negrín's continuously stated desire for resistance, when other Republican figures were looking for a negotiated solution, made him appear to be a communist sympathizer, if not an outright puppet; but he was his own man, dominating as no one had done before him politics in the Spanish Republic. In defiance of the communists, Negrín engaged in the search for a negotiated solution to the war, but did so – rightly – through private channels, in order not to affect the morale of the troops and the civilian population.

4.2 THE CONTAINMENT OF REVOLUTION

For the first few months of the war the Republic reeled from constant attacks on its authority. The army was abolished and much of the police force was lost. The courts were closed, with judges and lawyers hiding in fear for their lives. The subsequent breakdown of law and order was complete. Bands of armed men roamed the country, from small southern villages to Barcelona and Madrid, rooting out alleged supporters of the rebellion and settling personal and political scores, including, of course, the old and ill-defined conflict with the Church. Many of these men – but not all – were anarchist *exaltados* from Barcelona and other urban centres, imposing the logic of class hatred in towns and neighbourhoods where they were relatively unknown. Nearly 7,000 members of the clergy, including 13 bishops, over 4,000 priests and seminarians, over 2,000 monks and friars and even 283 nuns, were killed in a variety of degrading ways in Spain, while church buildings were destroyed in their hundreds. This was the worst massacre of Catholic clergy in history, and a demonstration of the scale and virulence of popular anticlericalism in Spain. Priests were universally regarded as having sided with the rebels and, whatever their actions in the face of events, assassinated. The strongly Catholic Basque Country provided a notable exception. Central and local authorities were impotent or unwilling to bring the killings to a halt, which undoubtedly contributed to the intensity of the Church's support for the rebels. All who could loosely be termed 'fascists' – right-wing supporters, Falangists, officers, policemen, employers and landowners – were also liable to be killed.

In the first days of war these crimes were not carried out by well-organized forces, but rather by spontaneously formed bands. With time, parties and unions developed their own police forces and makeshift courts in an attempt to re-establish order in the wake of the Republic's seeming demise, and these then took over the process of identifying and punishing the 'collaborators' with the rising. This was not a sound recipe for the immediate restoration of the due process of law. The indiscriminate terror did not disappear, being merely replaced by kidnappings at night and the ubiquitous *paseos* (car rides to a quiet area), which resulted equally in violent death. In the revolutionary atmosphere of July 1936, proving one's innocence before a party or union court – even if one was sufficiently fortunate to appear before such a body – was a difficult matter. José Rodríguez Olazábal, a magistrate in Valencia, described the local militia court, the Comité de Salud Publica, in frightening tones, claiming that it accentuated the terror felt in the city: 'Its agents would burst into private residences at any hour of the day or night, detained whomsoever they desired – civilian or military – and entered jails freely, from which they removed as many prisoners as they wanted' (Rodríguez Olazábal 1996: 73). According to the same author, over 3,000 people were killed for political motives in Valencia in the early weeks of the war. The government responded as it could. The temporary appointment of new judges began under the leadership of José Giral. In the wake of the assault on the Model Prison in Madrid in August 1936, popular tribunals were created, involving political parties and unions, who provided jurors, in the judicial process, in order to make it more open and acceptable in the new circumstances. However, it was not just the militias that undermined the authority of the Republic. Locally, power passed to popular committees made up of all present 'anti-fascist' parties while, regionally, official bodies like the Generalitat and the quickly agreed-to Basque government began to claim for themselves more power than they legally enjoyed. In Catalonia, regional and revolutionary bodies competed for power. The Generalitat was initially over-shadowed by Barcelona's Committee of the Anti-Fascist Militias. Lluys Companys, realizing that his 5,000 policemen could do little against 30,000 armed anarchists, offered his and his administration's services to the CNT/FAI. Not wanting at the time to involve them-selves in government, the anarchists accepted the offer. In Valencia, a Popular Executive Committee made up of the Popular Front parties and organizations took full control of the city; in Malaga, the same functions were taken up by the Comité de Salud Pública; there was a War Committee in Gijón, an Oviedo Provincial Committee and endless smaller variations. Two thousand towns printed their own money. Giral, aghast but powerless, could do nothing but recognize the legality of bodies for which there was no provision in the Constitution. There was no attempt by the CNT, however, to coordinate the action of these committees, for anarchists were loath to recreate the state apparatus, even if in their own image, neglecting as well to seize control of banking and financial institutions. It is generally agreed that the anarchists' failure to formalize these new local power structures, providing them with a common orientation, undermined their attempted revolution. Abroad, Spain's image, hurt by stories of indiscriminate terror and breakdown in authority, was further undermined by her diplomats, most of whom joined the Nationalist cause, in a series of highly public and damaging desertions.

Why did the various forces which nominally defended the Republic pursue such different aims in the summer of 1936, as the fighting intensified? First, because they underestimated the strength of their enemy, not realizing the impact that foreign intervention might have in Spain; indeed, the scale and the swiftness with which German and Italian military aid reached the rebels surprised everyone. More importantly, however, there were decades of accumulated rivalries that burst forth once the Republic found itself without a loyal army. Catalan and Basque separatists saw the disturbances as a chance to increase their power within the overall Spanish context. Lluys Companys, on 31 July 1936, styled himself president of Catalonia, and not, as before, of the Generalitat; he also spoke both of the need to create a Barcelona–Bilbao axis and for the interests of all 'Iberian peoples' (which, of course, implied that the Catalans formed an independent nationality) to be heard on vital matters such as the future of the Moroccan protectorate. This new-found ambition, which caused much anger in Madrid, was clear in the military action undertaken unilaterally by the Barcelona authorities, which Madrid-based Republicans liked Manuel Azaña interpreted as an ill-disguised attempt to build a 'Greater Catalonia'. Catalan military columns invaded areas of historic significance to Catalonia, such as Aragon and the Balearic Islands, while the threat to Madrid from Franco's armies grew.

Anarchists had long worked to destroy the bourgeois state, replacing its institutions and practices with unions and collectives that would deal directly with each other, having abolished the money economy. Many anarcho-syndicalists viewed July 1936 as an unparalleled opportunity to make their vision come true, whatever the CNT's national leadership might say about the importance of first winning the war. In the streets of anarchist-controlled towns and cities, modes of dress and address were proletarianized; jewels and other luxury items vanished, as did ties and hats, and restaurants became union-run canteens. The longstanding and often violent rivalry between the anarcho-syndicalist trade union, the CNT, and its socialist counterpart, the UGT, was also significant. Both movements carved out spheres of influence for the benefit of their memberships, which grew rapidly as individuals sought out the political and economic security of belonging to a union. Union membership facilitated access to food, medical care and housing. In Barcelona, the people having armed themselves in the wake of the rebels' defeat, large and small industrial concerns were collectivized, as were the shops of traders, craftsmen and service providers such as barbers and hairdressers. Rural collectives were also created throughout Spain, especially in areas where the CNT could demonstrate its strength unchecked, such as in the province of Aragon, where three-quarters of the land was collectivized: 450 collectives, involving 430,000 peasants, were formed. Many of these collectives were created forcibly by armed columns which set out from Barcelona. Popular with landless peasants, the notion of collectivization was as feared during the war by smallholders as it had been during the peacetime Republic (when, as we saw, it was a spectre that turned the CEDA into a mass party). Failure to act in a visibly radical manner in the city or in the country might lead to accusations of collusion with the old order being made by more extreme factions within the anarchist movements or revolutionary Marxist parties such as the Partido Obrero de Unificación Marxista (POUM). Strongest in Catalonia, the POUM also had its own militia. Many aspects of the defence of the Republic were harmed by this revolutionary drive. The first was the Republic's image abroad, hopelessly tarnished by atrocity stories and the fear that a second Bolshevik state was being created, whose example might sweep across Western Europe. With foreign correspondents based in major cities held by the Republic, or in Gibraltar, to which British citizens in the south of the country fled, the first stories concerning the war to reach the rest of the world concerned crazed 'Marxist' or 'Red' militias and their mindless killing sprees. Conservative newspapers in the rest of Europe deliberately ignored the subtleties of Republican politics, lumping together all factions, including moderate republicans loyal to Azaña, under the misleading term of 'Red'. This view was to last until the war's end in 1939, forcing the Republic's foreign propaganda to define repeatedly precisely what the Republic was and what it stood for, rather than concentrating its fire on the Nationalists, their goals and their crimes. It took a long time for the Republic to bring an end to the pointless killings; on 23 August 1936, for example, a fire in the Model Prison in Madrid, started in confused circumstances, led to a massacre of seventy political prisoners which the government was powerless to prevent. In September the anarchist 'Iron Column' invaded Valencia, taking over the local courthouse; its men proceeded to destroy archives and symbols of the justice system, such as robes, before turning the building into the FAI's headquarters. In November 1936 the evacuation of Madrid's prisons, supervised by Santiago Carrillo, secretary general of the JSU and councillor for public order in the Madrid Defence Junta, led directly to the shooting of 2,000 prisoners outside the capital.

The second way in which revolutionary activity hurt the war effort can be found in the effect that collectivizations and the attempt to destroy the existing capitalist economic order in Spain had on the Republic's war economy. It is worth remembering that the industrial centres of the country remained in Republican hands after the coup, and that in what was a modern war such a fact should have led to a more regular supply of arms for the Republican forces. Yet disorganization prevailed, and the efforts to turn all existing industrial capacity to the manufacturing of arms and munitions were usually unsuccessful. Precious time was lost while collectivized enterprises struggled to continue existing production, only to lose important foreign orders and discover that without credit they were doomed. The Generalitat did not help matters by legalizing the forty-hour week. In essence, the lack of a centralizing force conducting the Republic's economic effort makes it almost impossible to speak of a war economy. Given the history of labour relations in Spain, improving the conditions of workers and their salaries, rather than converting industry to meet the needs of an army which for the moment did not even exist, was understandably the priority of the collectivized industries. The vigour with which they pursued these wage demands, however, frustrated even the unions' leadership. This was a short-sighted policy, considering the gravity of the situation. Catalonia's industrial output was always to remain below pre-war levels, despite pressing needs and limited successes, such as the production of ammunition: by February 1937, half a million rifle cartridges were being produced monthly, despite the previous lack of any such production in the city. It is worth noting that this shortfall in production was also present in the Basque Country, where industry was not collectivized, which raises questions about the Basque government's ability and desire to organize its own war economy. In Catalonia technicians and trained staff, earning little more than unqualified workers, naturally gave little support to collectivization. The collectivization of industry not only affected the performance of the armies at the front, it increased the reliance of the Republic on Soviet military aid. Because of its infrequency and political implications – specifically, the favouring of the PCE – this aid was highly problematical. Political infighting for the control of industry should have given way, for the sake of the war effort and the desired victory over the Nationalists, to the rational and methodical exploitation of all available resources. The revolution made this impossible.

4.3 NON-INTERVENTION

The Republic's image abroad was harmed by the outburst of revolutionary violence that greeted the military rising, and, conversely, the failure to secure concrete aid from the Western democracies contributed, domestically, to the undermining of the Republican regime. What was the advantage of being a democratic republic if other similar countries did not come to Spain's rescue? Had the government been able to purchase arms and ammunition from France and Great Britain, its ability to restore order internally, not to mention defeat the rebels, would have been strengthened; as it turned out the internal situation took over a year to remedy. Paralyzed by the fear of a resurgent Germany under Hitler, and trying to appease Mussolini so as not to drive him into an alliance with Germany, Britain opted not to intervene in Spain, effectively reducing both sides – legitimate government and rebellious army – to the same moral level. That being the case, the French, who, under the leadership of socialist prime minister Léon Blum, had begun to supply the Republic with arms in July, proposed a policy of non-intervention, which was to prove a source of humiliation and frustration to successive Republican governments. Foreign representatives were invited to sign up to the principles of non-intervention, agreeing not to arm either side or send troops to the conflict, and thereby denying the Republic the means with which to defend itself from its internal enemy. Worse still, Germany and Italy repeatedly broke their pledge, sending men and weapons to aid Franco, and only the USSR responded in kind, allowing the Spanish Republic to buy arms. By early October, Soviet ships laden with weapons, including the impressive T-26 tank and the I-16 fighter, the fastest in Europe, had begun to pass through the Bosphorus on their way to Spain. Britain and France watched in cynical detachment as non-intervention developed into an entirely fictitious concept whose sole purpose was to help prevent a European war by allowing different policies to be pursued in Spain without fear of recrimination. An embittered Azaña was to write in May 1937 that 'our greatest enemy so far has been the British government'. The sole explanation the Spanish president could find for Britain's stance was that London desired strategic control of the whole of the Iberian peninsula, in accordance with which Azaña predicted that the British government would slowly improve its relations with Franco (Azaña 1990: 609). The Non-Intervention Committee, which first met in London on 9 September 1936, and before which Republican Spain could not appear, also deprived the League of Nations of any significant role in the crisis (which is not to say that the League would have been automatically favourable to the Republic, for only a minority of its members were liberal democracies). Spanish appeals for action by the authorities in Geneva, repeated throughout the war, were merely referred to the Committee, where, invariably, due to German, Italian and Portuguese action, and British and French appeasement, they were ignored. The words of Lloyd George to the Commons on 28 October 1937 remain today a powerful indictment of the Franco-British position: 'The fact of the matter is . . . that this committee of Non-Intervention is the greatest and basest fraud and deception ever perpetrated by great nations upon a weak people.' Even Negrín's unilateral withdrawal of foreign volunteers from the Republic's fighting forces in October 1938 was essentially ignored by the non-intervention signatories.

The Republic attempted from the start to regain its prestige and authority, a process which was naturally slow given the strength of the competing factions and the need to concentrate on fighting the increasingly efficient Nationalist forces. This process was made even more difficult by the disappearance of many leading republican politicians and officials in the aftermath of the rising. Frightened by the revolutionary excesses all over Spain, they made private arrangements and left for France. The Republic was thus left without committed doctrinal republicans to defend it, a source of frequent complaint by the ever-more isolated Azaña. Some forces, though, understood the need for a strong central authority able to coordinate the war effort and to create the stability necessary for victory. Their task was made easier by the CNT's unwillingness to guide the actions of the revolutionary committees that had sprung up throughout Republican Spain, transforming itself, in other words, into a national political force. Among these centralizing forces stood the reformist wing of the PSOE, led by Indalecio Prieto, and the PCE, both of which engaged in a struggle against the CNT, the POUM and, eventually, Largo Caballero. There was an important difference between the two, however: while Prieto's followers had always been committed to the Republic, seeing in it a regime capable of bringing about the gradual transformation of Spanish society that they desired, communist support was a new and essentially tactical development. Spanish communists received their strategic orientation from Moscow through the Communist International (Comintern), whose most capable operatives were rushed to Spain in 1936. The PCE's support for the Republic was part of the wider strategy of the Popular Front through which Stalin hoped to create and secure a great anti-fascist coalition that might protect the USSR from German attack. Thus the communists worked to return Spain to bourgeois normality (which meant the crushing of the collectives and of revolutionary committees) so that it might attract British and French support, leading to a crystallization of Europe into two blocks: in one the USSR and the Western democracies; in the other the fascist states. Stalin needed only to prolong the war, not to see the Republic win it, in order to bring about his desired diplomatic realignment. Domestically, the PCE's stance was presented as the consequence of the failure of the Spanish bourgeoisie to carry out its own historical task – the creation of a working parliamentary democracy. No disagreement was to be tolerated.

4.4 THE CRUCIAL ROLE OF THE PCE

In the aftermath of the Republican defeat, and in the context of the Cold War, the Communist Party's role in the Spanish Civil War was to be presented in a simplistic manner. Spanish communists were portrayed as mere puppets of Stalin, whose lack of trust in their nominal allies in the Popular Front eventually led to the downfall of the Republic. It was obvious, for example, that communist ministers had a strict policy line that they tried to impose on the cabinet; anarchist ministers, on the other hand, were content to carry out their tasks as best they could without receiving constant instructions from the CNT–FAI. However, more recent analysis has shown the vital role played by the communists in mobilizing support for the Republican regime at a time when republican and socialist parties were discredited by their failure to contain the rising and its aftermath. Communists attracted both the working and middle classes with the promise of victory through discipline, union and the preservation of order and property. The PCE, a small party in February 1936 (with a mere seventeen deputies in the Cortes), claimed 250,000 members by December 1936. Its dependent organizations played a crucial role in the mobilization of support from youth, women, small businessmen, traders, craftsmen and farmers around economic order and the Republic's basic principles and against the CNT's social experimentation. The Republic in Spain faced a terrible paradox. Its greatest and ablest supporter, the PCE, was readily identifiable with an isolated foreign power, the USSR, and its undeniably sectarian methods – including the unwavering attempt to control top political, administrative and military positions – were often unacceptable to other members of the Popular Front. The PCE allowed itself, for example, to become the Spanish arm of Stalin's purges of Old

Bolsheviks and their disciples, and permitted the creation in Spanish territory of Soviet prisons, over which the Spanish government had little control. In this way the POUM, whose leaders had personal connections with Leon Trotsky, and whose militia had been fighting the rebels since the first days of the war, was crushed under the guiding hand of Moscow. The communists' tactics, their contradictory appeals for support from all sectors of society, and the crude and simplistic nature of the propaganda the PCE directed towards the rural and urban working class were distasteful to the old-fashioned and elitist PSOE. The resulting hostility between the two parties constituted a serious breach in the unity of the Popular Front. Nevertheless, communists played a key role in the creation of the Popular Army, providing it with a model unit, the Fifth Regiment (later renamed Fifth Corps), which attracted 6,000 men in its first ten days of existence. The PCE played an essential role in the incorporation of the militias, which had shown their inability to contain the Nationalist forces in open battle, into the new national force. In this task they were greatly aided by both Soviet support and the apparent indifference of Britain and France to the Republic's fate. Close coordination between Soviet authorities and the PCE ensured that communist-led units received the most modern equipment, making them stronger than the militias and placing them at the centre of both fighting and intense propaganda activity. Elements of the ever-expanding Fifth Regiment were incorporated into former militia units, creating the mixed brigades that became the standard formation of the Popular Army, which eventually integrated even the POUM and CNT militias. The Fifth Regiment's command structure, which included political commissars alongside traditional officers, was reproduced throughout the whole Popular Army. Soviet funds and advice also poured into this propaganda campaign, so that the message of the communists obscured that of rival parties and organizations.

The PCE benefited from the prestige conferred by the International Brigades, military units organized by the Comintern whose volunteers were overwhelmingly communist. This willingness of Europe's communists to fight in Spain presented a clear contrast with the neutral stance of socialists and liberals. This committed and disciplined defence of the Republic, combined with Soviet aid and the PCE's undoubted discipline, proved very attractive to many, especially in the fragmented Socialist Party, who looked for a strong line against the enemy and the contending armed factions within the Republican zone. These 'fellow travellers' – men like the Foreign Minister Julio Alvarez del Vayo – would do much to implement the communist line. The communists also attracted the support of all those in the Republican zone who feared the excesses of the anarchist-led revolution and desired a return to normality. With Vicente Uribe in control of the Ministry of Agriculture, they distributed the land of the military rising's supporters while reining in the collectivist movement by supporting the claims of small farmers, to whom land was returned. At the same time, JSU work brigades in the countryside provided help to those farmers who chose independence rather than collectivization. In Catalonia the communists succeeded in fusing their party with the local socialists, thereby creating the Partit Socialista Unificat de Catalunya (PSUC), which grew into the most influential political force in the region. The PSUC acted as a loyal political wedge against the CNT and the POUM, and the communists attempted to complete this fusion in the rest of Spain, absorbing the PSOE. There was one flaw in the PCE's massive expansion: many of its new members were in the party out of immediate material considerations, and continued loyalty was dependent on the success of communist designs, including, naturally, the war itself.

4.5 THE MAY DAYS IN BARCELONA, 1937

The tensions which strained the Republic came to a head in the spring of 1937, as the Basque Country tried in vain to defend itself. The Basques were in an unenviable situation in Spain. As no social revolution had taken place within the Basque Country, and the Church continued to hold its important position among the people, they were seen with distrust by the rest of the Republic. It was the Republic's recognition of Basque autonomy and its respect for the Basque language and local rights and traditions that more than anything else brought Basque nationalists into the pro-Republic coalition, within which they stood out for their obvious conservatism.

Franco and the military rebels had no intention of allowing this regional autonomy to take root. José Antonio Aguirre, the newly instated Basque president, had to raise a nationalist militia of 30,000 *gudaris* – as the Basque soldiers were known – with which he hoped not only to protect his homeland, taking over from the socialist, communist and anarchist militias which had initially defended its borders, but to prevent assassinations, seizures of property and the burning of churches. As was the case with other militias, however, Basque officers were essentially amateurs and had little artillery and air power with which to counter the Nationalists. Too little was done by the rest of Republican Spain to help them.

Having been frustrated in his attempt to take Madrid early in 1937, Franco turned his revitalized forces against Bilbao, and instead of coming to the defence of the embattled Basques, whose industry was crucial to its prospects of victory, the Republic tore itself apart. In Barcelona, where tensions between revolutionary and centralizing factions had been mounting for days, the Generalitat's police tried to occupy the central telephone exchange, which was in the hands of the CNT, whose members could thus tap conversations of all kinds. Popular resistance to the police action led to the infamous May Days, which in many ways were the pivotal event in the Republicans' war. They were made possible by several currents of antagonism that undermined the Republic even as the state recovered its strength. The CNT's weak central organization, represented in the Spanish and Catalan governments, was trying to preserve what it could of the 1936 revolution in the face of the clear need for a united and massive effort against Franco and of the superior strength of the forces loyal to the bourgeois Republic. The anarchist grass roots, however, saw matters differently. For them, the increasing strength of the Spanish state – and of the Generalitat – signalled the return to the Republic of 1931, to which they owed little allegiance. Already, the re-establishment of normal food supply mechanisms under the Generalitat had led to the end of the requisitions in the countryside that had assured adequate food supplies for the workers of Barcelona. In line with decrees from Madrid an increasingly confident police force was disarming workers in the rearguard, while the Ministry of Finance's own police force, the Carabineros, on the orders of Juan Negrín, was engaged in shoot-outs with CNT patrols guarding the border with France. The PSUC's press added to the tension, carrying out daily and vicious attacks on the CNT, which it blamed for Catalonia's economic difficulties. The police assault on the telephone exchange was the last straw for the CNT rank and file, who, with little or no direction from above, took to the streets to protect their revolution. The assault was followed by two days of shooting between the anarchist and POUM militias – fighting to stave off what they saw as communist-inspired counter-revolutionary action – and the Catalan police, anxious to demonstrate that the Generalitat was strong enough to keep order in its capital city without the national government having to intervene. National anarchist leaders appealed for calm, while President Manuel Azaña, by then residing in Barcelona, barricaded himself in his palace and appealed for help from the government in Valencia.

The consequences of this embarrassing episode, in which 500 people died and 1,000 were wounded, were far-reaching: momentary military paralysis, which doomed the Basque Country; a renewal of party hatreds, which would result in the all-out attack against the POUM and contribute to the climate of hostility against the PCE; an increased presence in Barcelona of the central government's security forces and the subordination of the Army of Catalonia to the pro-communist General Sebastián Pozas; and, most importantly, the collapse of Largo Caballero's Popular Front government under strong communist pressure. The communist case against the prime minister had been prepared since the fall of the southern city of Malaga in February 1937. Largo and the PCE had been locked since then into an increasingly open battle for control of the top positions in the army and the power to appoint its political commissars. The communists also accused the prime minister of being reluctant to curb the idiosyncratic nature of the militias, preferring them to the mass conscript force which, the communists believed, was necessary to defeat Franco, and of moving too slowly against rural collectives. When Largo refused to punish the POUM and the CNT for their responsibility in the May Days, as the PCE had demanded, the two communist ministers walked out of the cabinet. Largo's days were numbered, since the temporary alliance between the PCE, the remaining republicans and Prieto's wing of the PSOE viewed Largo as expendable now that the CNT had been tamed. Orthodox republicans and *Prietistas* made it clear that they would not serve in a cabinet of which the communists were not a part. Defeated polit-ically, Largo was totally lost to the Republic's war effort under the lengthy premiership of his successor, Negrín.

The anarchists, for their part, were outraged by the ongoing attack on collectivization and by the communists' stance as defenders of the old bourgeois order; they refused to join Negrín's government, in which they were offered only two cabinet positions. In June the CNT also withdrew from the Generalitat. Clashes between the communists and anarchists were frequent as a struggle for control of Aragon followed the May Days. The Council of Aragon, which had functioned almost as the anarchist-inspired government of an independent state under the leadership of Joaquín Ascaso, was dissolved on 11 August 1937 and replaced by a governor general; Ascaso himself was arrested on the charge of jewel smuggling. Anarchists resisted the incorporation of their columns into the Popular Army as far as they could, but the leadership of the CNT understood the need to win the war, and, within the context of the Republican zone, its own ultimate military weakness. This logic impelled it to accept the transformation of the old anarchist columns into divisions of the Popular Army, under centralized command.

The socialists and the anarchists were sufficiently strong to defend themselves from the PCE and its aggressive approach. The same could not be said for the small POUM, which after the May Days became the target of communist fury, leading to the closing of offices and newspapers, the disbanding of the Twenty-ninth Division (the old POUM militia) and the arrest of the party's leadership. The POUM had allowed itself to become friendless in Republican Spain. Republicans and socialists viewed its revolutionary stance with distrust and dislike. To the communists, the POUM was a hotbed of Trotskyist dissent that had to be eliminated. In the communist press the POUM's supporters were described as covert fascists intent on sabotaging the Republican war effort. Even the CNT saw the small party as a rival for control of the Catalan working class. A later trial would find charges of treason brought against the party's leadership to be groundless, but this came too late to save the leading figure of the POUM, Andrés Nin, from torture and death at the hands of the Soviet secret police. This was another event which sapped the will to fight in Republican Spain, not out of love for Nin and the POUM, but out of the fear that the communists were indeed taking over the state's apparatus, becoming a law unto themselves, and that the Republic's victory would in essence be the PCE's victory and no one else's. The official explanation eventually advanced for Nin's disappearance – that he had been sprung from jail by false German International Brigaders and delivered to their common fascist paymasters – raised more questions than it answered, and was largely disbelieved.

4.6 REPUBLICAN NORMALITY UNDER JUAN NEGRÍN

As the war wore on, both before and during Negrín's government, the Republic became better organized, the orders from the government and the High Command being obeyed at the front. A resumption of law and order occurred, with a new judicial device – the popular tribunals – being erected and made acceptable to all parts, and a strong and well-armed police force active in the rear. There were occasional embarrassments, such as the declaration of independence by the doomed Council of Asturias on 28 August 1937, opposed only by the local communists, and its dismissal of the military commanders appointed by the central government, but these tended to disappear as the war entered its second year. Increased centralization, and the much reduced role allotted to the Cortes in wartime, also allowed for government stability: Negrín's power was unchallenged, and a brief ministerial crisis in August 1938 showed the complete lack of rivals for the leadership of the Republican government. It is often stated that this centralization, and the resulting curbing of the anarchist revolution, came at a price: lower morale among many army units, increased political infighting and, once victory appeared to have slipped definitively from the grasp of the Republicans, the notion that only the communists kept the war alive. This may well have been the case, but these accusations have not yet been satisfactorily quantified; it seems more logical to consider the fall of morale as a consequence both of a long series of military defeats and of an ever-worsening crisis of supplies. The truth was that in the face of the international support received by Franco, the Republic's internal politics meant little; this much was recognized by, for example, Manuel Azaña, who by the autumn of 1937 had become convinced that the war was lost.

The last great political victory of the PCE took place in April 1938, as Franco's armies were dashing to the Mediterranean and the government moved from Valencia to Barcelona to be nearer to the French border. That month the communists managed to obtain the removal of Indalecio Prieto from his position as war minister, successfully pinning the responsibility for successive military defeats on Prieto's infamous pessimism. A popular demonstration led by Dolores Ibárruri – better known as La Pasionaria – on 16 March 1938 interrupted a cabinet meeting and called for Prieto's removal. Prieto and Azaña were shocked by the crude nature of the scapegoating tactics employed by the PCE, but eventually had to give in.

Just as the control of the army's top positions and the commissariat had brought the communists into conflict with Largo Caballero, so too did it drive a wedge between them and Prieto (and by 1938 the clash was made worse by the struggle to control the Army Intelligence Service, the SIM). Both socialist leaders had also been alarmed by the communists' desire for amalgamation with the PSOE. Negrín assumed the defence portfolio after Prieto's departure from the cabinet, but he did so at the cost of becoming more isolated from his party, which was increasingly wary of the communists' tactics and aims. From that moment normal relations between Negrín and Prieto became impossible, and Negrín's internal position much more dependent than before on the immediate success of his overall strategy.

As the Republic's last throw of the dice, the Ebro Battle, gave way to a Nationalist invasion of Catalonia and the fall of Barcelona, the end of the fighting was increasingly desired for many reasons. First, the price of victory now seemed too high: more and more territory was coming under the rule of Franco; the Republic's cities were routinely and with impunity bombed from the air; millions of displaced Spaniards lived as refugees; and hunger had become a generalized ordeal. The majority of the population in the Republican zone was exhausted by the war. That the war could be brought to an end if a break with the PCE was achieved was an idea that took a long time to germinate, but burst open violently after the fall of Barcelona. When on 10 February 1939 Negrín returned to the Madrid front by air, he intended to carry on with a war that to all observers seemed lost, or to negotiate a peace according to the three conditions he had presented to the last meeting in Spain of the Republican Cortes. This session had been held in the border town of Figueras on 1 February 1939 in the presence of only sixty-two deputies. The three conditions were the preservation of Spain's independence, freedom from persecution for political and military activities during the war and the right of Spaniards to choose their form of government. The communists' objection to a negotiated peace, familiar to all in the Republican zone, was easy to understand: they feared becoming the sacrificial lamb with which Republicans and socialists appeased Franco. By proclaiming his intention to fight on, Negrín was unfairly identified as a puppet of the communists, and, therefore, an obstacle to peace. One can question, however, Negrín's ability to gauge public opinion, rising above Republican war propaganda to establish how the population felt about the war after the fall of Barcelona.

Many doubts were kept alive by defeated Republicans in exile. Among these the possibilities of success of a truly revolutionary war, as advocated by anarchists and the POUM, played a significant part. Starting from the admission that the Nationalists had a stronger professional army, might not the adequate response have been to favour the militias and the popular characteristics of the war, adopting, for example, the guerrilla tactics that over a century earlier had driven Napoleon's generals to despair? Considering the popular enthusiasm and loyalty that the CNT could generate, might not a constant drive to collectivize agriculture and industry have provided the sheer numbers of committed soldiers with which to overwhelm the enemy? Questions such as these and futile accusations of incompetence and betrayal rendered the lives of Republican exiles even more bitter, and would ensure that they never spoke as one in order to mount effective political opposition to Franco. Such an opposition would have to develop in Spain itself over the space of decades. One fact seems indisputable, however: the communists, in repressing the revolutionary elements of the Popular Front – the POUM and, to a much lesser extent, the CNT – reinforced the power of those moderate forces which had distrusted their own ability to win the war from the very first moment. After all, had it not been for the CNT and sectors of the UGT, the Martínez Barrio compromise solution sketched out in July 1936 might have been more successful. Popular enthusiasm was ignored in the attempt to recreate bourgeois normality; it is, of course, impossible to say that the reverse would have led to a different military outcome. In any case, some have questioned the depth of this popular enthusiasm for the revolutionary cause, even in the city of Barcelona, arguing that much of it was faked to improve personal circumstances.

Did the revolution cost the Republic the war? The answer seems to be that foreign intervention – and non-intervention – ultimately did more damage to the Republican war effort. The total abdication by Great Britain and France of their responsibility, as dictated by the principles of collective security, was short-sighted. The League of Nations was understandably wary of becoming engaged in a civil war, but foreign intervention in Spain had completely transformed the conflict. It prevented the Republic from curbing revolutionary excesses and it could very well have had much more serious consequences during the Second World War, had Franco decided to join Hitler and Mussolini in 1940. Conversely, the constant arrival of foreign *matériel* for the Nationalists was demoralizing. Whatever improvement the Popular Army made to its fighting ability was always, in the end, countered and bested by the Nationalists. Moreover, while the Republic's monetary reserves had to go towards arms, food, energy and medical supplies, all of which had to be paid for in cash, Franco was allowed to borrow whatever sums were necessary to prosecute the war, mortgaging Spain's future prosperity. In many ways the scale of foreign intervention renders the designation of Spanish Civil War misleading. The Republic was hampered in its attempt to defend itself and was denied its rights as a legitimate regime and as a member of the League of Nations. Its leaders had not been intransigent or stubborn; even Negrín had been open to a negotiated settlement, developing contacts with the Vatican, German diplomats and figures within the Nationalist camp. None of these initiatives met with any success in the face of Franco's absolute refusal to accept anything other than unconditional surrender. The full extent of the Republic's nightmare situation was made clear on 16 April 1938 when the British government, now led by Chamberlain, signed a pact for Mediterranean stability with Italy, by which Italy agreed to withdraw all of its troops from Spain once the war there had ended – this while the policy of non-intervention was still in place, and its committee continued to meet in London. Against this duplicitous attitude there was little that Negrín could do.

CHAPTER FIVE

The Nationalists' war

Two factors allowed the Nationalists to win the Spanish Civil War. The first was massive foreign intervention in their favour; the second was their unity of command and of purpose. Unity of purpose was not just the initial collegial solidarity of the officer corps that rebelled in 1936. It was achieved by fusing together, through a variety of means, the political parties and factions that had been willing to engage in the fight against the Republic, destroying the independence and initiative of their respective leaderships without alienating the mass of supporters. This difficult task was achieved by Franco and his closest associates by concentrating minds on the task at hand – winning the war – while remaining enigmatic on the subject of what political path postwar Spain would take. Falangists, Carlists, Alfonsist monarchists: all could hope during the conflict that after victory their political ambitions would triumph. The truth was, however, that bereft of an independent leadership, and as a result of policies dictated by the wartime need for secrecy and security, no views could be made public by politicians of these tendencies save through organs controlled by the army and, of course, by Franco, who sat atop all hierarchies as head of state, commander of the armed forces and leader of the sole unified party permitted in the country. The Nationalist victory in 1939 would have been impossible if the political dissension which plagued the Republic's defence had also manifested itself in Francoist Spain. At times it seemed that this might indeed happen, and the Republic's leaders were often encouraged by the power struggles which took place in Nationalist Spain, releasing imprisoned political figures – especially Falangists – whom they thought might complicate matters further. However, both the hatred of the Republic's leadership common to all members of the Nationalist coalition and their shared complicity in the massive repression that accompanied Nationalist territorial expansion were strong enough to allow Franco to keep fighting without serious distractions in his rearguard.

5.1 FROM COUP TO CIVIL WAR

As the coup escalated into a civil war, the army required the ever-greater participation of civilian volunteers, who were naturally drawn from the political parties of the right (later still conscription would be introduced). When looked at generally, the aims of the various groups that made up this new Nationalist coalition were quite diverse. There were those who merely wished to reform the Republic by purging it of elements they deemed to be 'undesirable', thinking that violence in Spain was a problem to be resolved and not a symptom of deeper complications – that violence was the action of terrorists who could only be dealt with by force, after which everything would return to 'normal'. Many who had supported the CEDA – undeniably a mass party – fell into this category, and it was to these more moderate supporters that Nationalist propaganda turned in order that their desire for peace should not obscure the need for complete victory. Others had more extreme views and accepted the logic of civil war with fewer scruples. The Falange wanted to replicate the Italian Fascist experience, adapting it to the different Spanish reality. Its surviving leadership, from the outbreak of the Civil War, dedicated itself to the tasks of strengthening the party's structure and mobilizing support for the conflict through the development of media organs, military academies and the provision of social services such as crèches and canteens. Although anachronistically imperialist, strictly authoritarian and Catholic (though some elements within the party were anticlerical, drawing a distinction between Christianity as a useful social doctrine and the Catholic Church as an institution), the Falange's programme contained at least a recognition that there were serious social ills in Spain, and that some redistribution of wealth would be necessary in order for these ills to be corrected. Point 9 of its programme stated that 'in the economic sphere, we think of Spain as one huge syndicate of all those engaged in production' (Kenwood 1993: 43). Point 19 committed the party to achieving 'a social organisation of agriculture' by 'redistributing once again all the arable land to promote family holdings and by giving farmers every encouragement to join the union' (ibid.: 45). The Falange also defended the introduction of a corporative structure in Spain and the creation of vertical unions grouping together employers and workers in each economic sector. This approach was ignored by the more conservative wings of the Nationalist alliance, which consisted of the Alfonsist monarchists who had lost their leader, Calvo Sotelo, immediately before the war, and the Carlists. Carlism's survival as a living ideology with popular appeal was a reflection of Spain's uniqueness in European politics. Modernized by an infusion of foreign thought, such as a desire for a corporative rearrangement of Spanish life, Carlism was rooted firmly in the nineteenth-century rejection of liberalism, and its commitment to a monarchy and militant Catholicism was complicated by an allegiance to a proscribed branch of the Spanish royal family. Carlism's appeal to the well-off Navarrese peasantry was undeniable, and thousands flocked to the movement's militia, the Requeté, when the uprising began, confidently marching on Madrid alongside regular army units only to be surprised by popular resistance in the mountains north of the capital.

In order to bring together this disparate coalition, Franco had to emphasize common points and stress constantly the need for victory over the Republic, whose leaders were depicted in an ever-worsening and more dehumanized fashion. By allowing – or, better still, forcing – factions to overcome the political differences that separated them, a common purpose was instilled. Support could be found by appealing for loyalty to the army and the Church, two institutions long seen as bulwarks of conservative Spain. A process of militarization took place, subordinating all party political interests to those of the army, which was greatly expanded as volunteers were accepted and new junior officers trained. In December 1936 Franco decreed the incorporation of all political militias into the army, placing their respective commanders at the orders of loyal officers. Following German advice, he embarked on the creation of a mass army, a process which took place in a far smoother way than in the Republic. In September 1936 courses were created for the training of reserve officers – the *alféreces provisionales* – which were open to men of twenty (later eighteen) to thirty years of age with a degree or professional qualifications. These reserve officers could rise to the rank of colonel. By the end of the war, twenty-two centres, with Spanish and

German instructors, had produced nearly 23,000 of these officers, whose training lasted a mere twenty-four days. Such hurried training limited the overall military value of these middle-class contributors to the war effort, but their enthusiasm was not in doubt, and they would prove themselves superior to their Republican equivalent. Unlike the Republic's Popular Army, the Nationalists could conduct offensive operations – even if following the simplest of tactics – with some confidence of success. By the spring of 1937 the Nationalist army stood at 200,000 men, and all told the Nationalists mobilized around a million Spaniards for their army.

Politics within the Nationalist camp were superficially less complicated than in the Republican zone. Franco followed the time-honoured techniques of dividing in order to rule, and of making himself indispensable to the contending camps: Falangists, Carlists, Alfonsists and the rest. The foreign press, meanwhile, described him as commander-in-chief of the Nationalist forces from the earliest days of the conflict, thanks to misinformation emanating from his headquarters. When Franco adopted the monarchist flag, his support was boosted among conservatives; yet this was an essentially empty gesture, which did not commit him to overseeing the restoration of the monarchy. The emergence of Franco as the absolute leader of the Nationalist camp was a rapid process. Foreign aid was channelled exclusively through Franco; he commanded the best troops, and his columns met with spectacular advances. The only civilian who might have rivalled him, after the death of Calvo Sotelo, was José Antonio Primo de Rivera; however, the leader of the Falange was to be executed in Alicante Jail on 20 November 1936. Despite the cult of José Antonio that he was to launch later, Franco rejoiced in private at the death of his rival. Other potential threats were swiftly dispatched. Don Juan de Borbón, son of Alfonso XIII, was prevented from serving in the Spanish navy as he had requested, Franco considering, for the benefit of monarchist opinion, the prince too important a figure in the country's future to risk death in action. Franco let it be known in Falangist circles, however, that he had deliberately kept the heir away to facilitate the creation of a Falangist state. Gil Robles, leader of the CEDA, was mercilessly attacked for his failure to seize power in the aftermath of the 1934 rebellion and eventually forced into exile by threats in the Falangist press. On 29 September the Carlist pretender, Don Alfonso Carlos, died without children. Finally, Manuel Fal Conde, political leader of the Carlists, was driven from Spain after creating a 'Royal Military Academy' for his Requeté in December 1936, despite the fact that the Falange had two such institutions for the formation of its officers. This last move preceded the subordination of political militias to the army, which naturally strengthened Franco's hand.

Formalizing the united political front was also an important step in the strengthening of the Nationalist war machine. The key figure in this respect was Franco's brother-in-law, Ramón Serrano Súñer, who, after his escape from Republican territory, quickly established himself as Franco's principal political adviser, replacing the Caudillo's inexperienced brother, Nicolás. A former leader of the JAP, Serrano Súñer understood the need not for a loose coalition of support, such as Primo de Rivera's old UP (an idea defended by Nicolás Franco), but for a strictly controlled political party sufficiently strong to quell internal dissent and sufficiently vague, in ideological terms, to allow all Nationalists to join. Such a party would leave no room for lawful political expression outside its sphere of influence. The Falange's numbers had increased massively by early 1937 (many of the new members having joined in order to hide a politically suspect past), and its fascist trappings facilitated relations with Italy and Germany. As a result it was ideally placed to be Franco's vehicle for mass political mobilization. Serrano Súñer's action in this field led to the April 1937 Decree of Unification, by which the absurdly named Falange Española Tradicionalista y de las Juntas de Ofensiva Nacional Sindicalista (FET y de las JONS) was brought into being, fusing together Carlists and Falangists. This piece of legislation signalled the creation of the Francoist political system, which would last until 1975. By this stage the most important Carlists had already been pushed aside, while the Falange, deprived of José Antonio Primo de Rivera, was equally vulnerable and split along lines of conflicting leadership claims. It is important to note that by this stage only the parties with considerable military strength were deemed worthy of being incorporated into the single party: the CEDA was a thing of the past. Manuel Hedilla, aged thirty-five, was the temporary leader of the Falange in April 1937, having been appointed by José Antonio himself. His leadership was contested, however, by the personal friends and relatives of José Antonio after the latter's death. These contending factions were no match for Franco's power and political guile, proving themselves incapable of preserving the old Falange's individuality in the face of Franco's bid for supreme control. Franco was imposed on the new party as Jefe Nacional. This was described as the sole compromise solution acceptable to all, but in reality Franco's candidacy was yet another step in his drive for total power in Spain since in the FET y de las JONS power resided not with its membership but, exclusively, with the leadership. Some attempts at a mutiny were sketched in the spring of 1937 but these were easily snuffed out.

Serrano Súñer became the practical leader of the party. Hedilla, after refusing an honorary position within the new structure, also refused to leave the country, being arrested on 25 April and charged with plotting against the state. The main body of the FET y de las JONS was its National Council, where forty-five men and three women sat and where old Falangists and Carlists were outnumbered by new entries, chosen only for their loyalty to Franco. The twenty-six points of the old Falange were adopted unquestioningly as the goals of the new party, which continued as a result to be acceptable to Germany and Italy. There was no actual commitment to a monarchist restoration under any branch of the royal family, merely the creation of an ordered, hierarchical and authoritarian state – a compromise acceptable to monarchists eager to crush the Republic. By the end of the war the FET y de las JONS had 650,000 members, proof of its success as a badge of approval for Franco's designs and of its power as a source of protection and patronage.

The increasing importance of the FET y de las JONS also allowed Franco to strangle, in a gradual way, the empire established by General Queipo de Llano in Seville since the beginning of the Civil War. Queipo, not content with fighting the war in the southern sector, had also presumed to legislate, introducing economic and social measures such as draining of marshes, financial aid to smallholders, improved housing for workers and developing industry in Seville – all while trying to foster a spirit of cooperation between capital and labour. In an ironic twist, Queipo distributed the land of Republican sympathizers to landless labourers. As Franco's power grew, Queipo's ability to interfere in politics declined. In January 1938 Franco turned the Junta Técnica del Estado, which helped him to rule the country, into a full government totally dominated by military figures of undisputed loyalty. The sole Falangist of the old school was the agriculture minister, Raimundo Fernández Cuesta, who had been released by the Republican government in an exchange of prisoners. A former secretary general of the party, his arrival in the Nationalist zone gave new hope to the party's veterans, but Fernández Cuesta soon demonstrated his subservience to Franco. As minister, his main policy was the return of land seized by or distributed to landless peasants to its former owners. By undoing the work of the Institute of Agrarian Reform, Fernández Cuesta gave a practical demonstration of how little emphasis the Nationalists actually placed on the social redistribution of land as detailed in the twenty-six points.

5.2 SECURING FRANCO'S POWER

In less than a year, therefore, Franco became Generalísimo, head of state with further responsibilities as chief of government and head of a unified single party, the FET y de las JONS, which absorbed all other political factions. His power, military and political, was unlimited. He had become the Caudillo, the providential leader come to save the country from its enemies. Franco was not a fascist. There is an element of revolutionary politics in fascism, of wanting to provoke a dramatic change in society. That was not Franco's intention: on the contrary, he wanted to preserve Spain from change, or even to return it to a mythical time when there was no regionalist feeling, when the Catholic Church dictated both social norms and the pace of intellectual progress, when the army was respected, and when the workers – in rural and urban areas – had no power. This was not fascism; but fascism in the 1930s was viewed by many as the political future of Europe and as an agent of modernization. Franco did not hesitate to borrow its trappings – single party, uniforms, rallies, the spirit of blind obedience in a leader – to suit his needs, only dropping the desire to revolutionize society. The Falange's social programme, although adopted as an official ideology, was never to be fully implemented, and no challenge was ever mounted against either private property or the rights of the Catholic Church and its control over education. In any case, the debate as to whether Franco was a fascist is in many ways irrelevant, since the denial of Franco's fascism has often been an essential part of attempts to legitimize his actions. The fact remains that his brutality matched or even exceeded that of Mussolini. Franco was an arch-reactionary and, above all else, he wanted to concentrate power in his own hands, making sure that victory would provide him with the legitimacy to rule Spain after the war. To turn the country into a replica of Italy would be to turn himself into a satellite of Mussolini, and this Franco refused to do. He was not taking power in order to become a subordinate to somebody else. This spirit of independence was to remain with him until his death. Hitler, after their 1940 meeting, stated that he would rather have three or four teeth pulled out than negotiate with Franco again – and this despite German aid in the Civil War and the fact that, after defeating France, Hitler had become the unquestioned master of Western Europe.

The attempt to provide Franco's rule with some legitimacy was made not only by his military peers and new political allies but also by the Catholic Church. The Church had been in retreat in Spain since 1931, when the Republic struck at the heart of its privileges and its pivotal social role. Amid the chaos and murder of the first months of the war, with anarchists controlling large swathes of territory, with authority breaking down and with the Soviet Union backing the Republic, the Church quickly made up its mind: this was not a common civil war. It was rather a crusade for Catholicism, a fight to the death between Spain's spiritual greatness and internationalist materialism. Catholic support would help to make the Nationalist message available and acceptable to a mass audience at home and abroad. Initial pastoral support was given by Bishop Enrique Plá y Deniel of Salamanca – the first churchman to describe the war as a crusade – whose lead was then followed by Cardinal Isidro Gomá and the rest of the Church's hierarchy. The climax of this Catholic support came in July 1937, when all but three Spanish bishops published a pastoral letter conveying their enthusiasm for the Nationalist cause. The prelates of Spain voiced their support for Franco at home and abroad, denouncing Republican atrocities but omitting to mention those committed by their own side. The Church also remained quiet on the subject of the Basques, who fought Franco in order to preserve their recently granted autonomy. In the Basque Country no rift had developed between the Church and the mass of the people, and yet the Basques fought on the side of the Republic: their very existence contradicted the notion of the crusade. Basque priests aiding their troops were shot by Franco's forces, but the Catholic hierarchy remained silent. The fact that in towns like Guernica civilians were deliberately targeted, confirming the longstanding predictions of the aeroplane as the destroyer of whole cities, was also ignored by the Church. In return for the Church's loyalty, Franco handed it control over the country's morals and education, from primary to tertiary level, backing its conservative views rather than the Falange's totalitarian intentions.

As can be expected, discipline was enforced thoroughly in Francoist Spain during the war. We have already seen that the use of terror was well understood by officers with an experience of the Moroccan conflict, and that terror was an inbuilt part of the strategy behind the rising. In the Spain of 1936 there were many for whom no reconciliation with the enemy was possible. Six generals and thirty-four Popular Front deputies were shot by the rebels as a prelude to their attempt to resolve decades of mounting social tension by force. The fear that Republican supporters behind the front line might later revolt naturally led to close surveillance, searches and the attempt to identify accurately personal political allegiances. In the heated political climate of Spain such searches resulted in violence. Thus, for example, landowners, upon the recapture of their estates by Nationalist forces, presented the army or the Falange militia with the names of workers who should be punished and shot. The language employed by the nascent Francoist state legitimized violent repression. The action of the army was described as a purging or a cleansing of Spanish society, which had been contaminated by anti-Spanish elements. Martial law was declared; all those opposed to the rising were, in a complete reversal of legal fact, deemed to be rebels. Repression was formalized: decrees established the penalties for opposing the Nationalist cause, which ranged from imprisonment and hard labour to death. Repression also acted as a 'pact of blood', making all Nationalist supporters collectively responsible for the atrocities committed in their name, and therefore unwilling to tolerate in the future a government that might inquire into their doings during the war. In the early phase of Franco's campaign when the rebels' hold over the country was still tenuous, the push from the south towards Madrid saw terror employed extensively in the southern cities. There were massacres in Seville (where up to 10,000 people were shot during the war), Córdoba (where mass executions took place despite the fact that the city had fallen to the rebels with almost no resistance) and Granada (up to 8,000 deaths) in order both to punish Republican sympathizers and to secure the rearguard. Once again use was made of Moroccans and the foreign legion against the Spanish population, in a replica of the 1934 Asturian campaign. This suggests that Franco and other Nationalist commanders viewed the Civil War as a colonial campaign, and their enemies as not being properly Spanish. After the capture of Almendralejo, 1,000 prisoners were shot, including 100 women. Two thousand were shot some days later when Badajoz fell to Yagüe. In February 1937 4,000 people would be killed in one week after the capture of Malaga. When Bilbao fell in June of the same year 1,000 executions took place. The toll was high everywhere.

Civil wars are often marked by greater brutality than international wars, and the Spanish case was no exception. The Nationalists, as a rule, no longer accepted any possibility of compromise; the Republic's supporters, for their part, were deeply divided over the use of terror, but their leadership at least acknowledged that one day the survivors of the two opposing camps would have to live together again. All in all, it is estimated that over 200,000 defenders, and suspected defenders, of the Republic were executed during or immediately after the war. With massacres on both sides, the question can be asked whether there was any difference between the two contending parties. The answer is that there was indeed a difference. The Republican governments struggled to bring an end to such actions, ultimately with success, subordinating punishment to a wartime, and therefore abbreviated, legal procedure. In this task they were aided by friendly political parties and trade unions, which sought to impose obedience on their respective memberships. Political power, once secured, was used to quell violence. Franco, however, encouraged terror and a lack of mercy both during and after the war: violence was for him a means to attain and secure power. Reconciliation was a forbidden subject in Nationalist Spain, a logical impossibility. What was taking place, the Nationalist leadership argued, was the sole course left open if Spain was to survive: purification through violence. This implacable attitude would be maintained until and beyond the end of the conflict. In February 1939, as the fall of Madrid approached, Franco armed himself legally with the power to deal with his real and suspected enemies in any way that he saw fit. This power was conferred by the Law of Political Responsibilities, published that month by Franco's government, which gave Franco a free hand in his final reckoning with the Republic. Even the failure to resist the Republic from as early as October 1934, described as 'grave passivity', was deemed to be a crime of rebellion. Most Spaniards were thus covered by the law's provisions. Evidence against individuals was admissible from all loyal sources in conditions that offered the suspects little ability to defend themselves.

5.3   FOREIGN AID TO THE NATIONALISTS

It is impossible to explain the reasons for the Nationalist victory without examining foreign aid to Franco. This aid arrived in Spain from the very first days of the war, and at crucial times was brought to bear on the Republicans, whose own supply of Soviet arms was more limited and less frequent. Foreign air power in the shape of German JU-52 transports allowed for the initial transfer of soldiers from Africa to Seville, securing western Andalusia as a bastion for the rebels. Foreign air power, combined with the intimidating presence of German warships, was also able to drive the Republican fleet from Moroccan waters, ensuring that a more efficient transfer of the Army of Africa could take place by sea. As early as 25 July 1936 Franco and his representatives in Italy had negotiated the supply of twelve bombers; that same day Hitler, in Bayreuth, entertained a similar Spanish delegation; four days later the first shipment of German transport planes and fighters was dispatched to Franco's rescue. From that moment on, foreign aid would play an ever-greater role in the course of the war. Nationalist soldiers, unlike their Republican counterparts, were seldom short of ammunition and, more significantly, rifles; alongside them fought regular Italian troops and Fascist Party militiamen, supported by modern artillery, tanks and aircraft, and the German Condor Legion, composed of air force, anti-aircraft and other specialized units. The Condor Legion's strength usually stood at 5,000 men in total, but these were frequently rotated; a much higher number of Germans served, in fact, in Spain, with estimates ranging from 12,000 to 30,000. The Italian 'Volunteer Corps' was a more substantial force, numbering over 70,000 men; another 4,000 flew and serviced Italian air force machines, while substantial aid was also provided on the seas. The regular officers who commanded these troops usually enjoyed good relations with the military leadership of Nationalist Spain: conservative or fascist Italian and German officers naturally understood and appreciated the Nationalist cause, if not necessarily Franco's leadership.

Why Mussolini and Hitler decided to intervene in Spain – and, in the Italian case, in such a massive fashion – must be considered. In the late 1930s Mussolini's Fascist state was driven, as a result of the Duce's failure to carry out radical transformations within Italian society, by the need for action and expansion abroad. Since its coming to power, Fascism had evolved into an aggressive form of nationalism which relied, for the calming of internal rumblings, on the prestige and the promise of financial gain to be derived from an expansionist foreign policy. There was very little room in Europe, however, for this outward drive, which had already been channelled at great diplomatic cost into the sole remaining independent African state, Abyssinia, conquered by Italy in 1936. Elsewhere Italy's growth was constricted by the presence of Britain and France, two larger and more powerful European and colonial rivals. Mussolini did not, however, despair of his position. He believed that the balance of power in Europe and, more specifically, in the Mediterranean, was turning, and that in the near future Italy's position could be improved. Spain was important to Mussolini because of its strategic position on the western end of the Mediterranean, which the dictator wanted to turn into an Italian lake. The two entrances to the Mediterranean were controlled by Great Britain, and a friendly Spain would do much to negate the influence of Gibraltar on Mediterranean strategy. Moreover, a friendly Spain would disrupt the transfer of French troops from Africa to Europe in a European war, rendering France weaker and therefore more amenable to a new diplomatic settlement with Italy. Indeed, this French dimension to the crisis was paramount to Mussolini. Should the Spanish Republic survive thanks to French military aid then, as a reward, French influence in Spain, especially over the Balearic Islands, might increase. This would be to the obvious detriment of Mussolini's grand strategy, in which France, as the weaker of his two rivals, was viewed as a more immediate target for aggression. However, when Mussolini realized that both the British government and French domestic opinion were preventing Léon Blum from coming to the aid of the Spanish Republic, he did not hesitate to send military supplies to Franco. For this decision he was applauded not only by the Fascist Party, eager for a military triumph for its blackshirted militia, but by the Catholic Church. The democracies' failure to come to the rescue of one of their number made Mussolini's dreams of Mediterranean hegemony come one step closer, and he acted with all possible speed.

Fascism, as an ultra-nationalist doctrine, could not brook defeat and survive. For that reason, Italian aid, once offered, could not be withdrawn before Franco had become master of Spain. Mussolini was trapped in a number of ways once his troops had landed in Spain. First and foremost was the nature of the war that Franco intended to fight by the time Italian 'volunteers' began to arrive. This was a slow campaign, without shortcuts or lightning advances, which gave people time to declare for or against the Republic. Such a declaration would then lead either to punishment or reward. On a number of occasions the war seemed to be as good as won, yet Franco's conception of the conflict allowed the Republic to recover its strength and continue fighting. This approach exasperated Mussolini, who could ill afford the price of his aid to Franco and for whom the war should have been fought in such a way as to bring about the quickest possible victory. Despite many threats to reduce or withdraw Italian aid, Mussolini was helpless in the hands of Franco; the war had to be fought Franco's way, whatever the views of the Italian generals present. The sensible Italian desire to advance along the Mediterranean coast, closing off the Republic's access to the sea, was ignored in favour of the lengthy and uncertain battles for control of Madrid and, once these had failed, the northern front. A second problem for Mussolini was that his army, despite being more modern than the Spanish forces it was fighting against, was not sufficiently proficient to tip the scales by itself. In some cases, especially after the arrival of Soviet weaponry, the Italians found themselves outgunned and outmanoeuvred. In March 1937 they were badly mauled at the Battle of Guadalajara, in winter conditions for which the men and their equipment were not prepared. This battle, thanks to which Madrid continued to be held in the hands of the Republic, was a terrible embarrassment to Italian Fascism. Mussolini could only respond by replacing his commanders on the field and committing even more troops to a campaign for which his enthusiasm had waned considerably.

Italian aid was the most significant for Franco's war effort in terms of numbers. Italy's intervention, for example, helped to save Mallorca from the invasion force sent by Catalonia in 1936. Mussolini was to provide the Nationalist war effort with 1,800 artillery pieces, 6,800 motor vehicles, 157 tanks and nearly 700 aeroplanes. Italian troops on the ground, however, did not add decisively to the strength of the Nationalist war machine. As significant, if not more so, because of the technological superiority it entailed, was the aid that arrived from Germany, both in terms of weapons for Franco's army and of German fighting units. German fighters, after the arrival of the Bf-109 in 1937, dominated the skies and ensured aerial supe-riority wherever they were based; German bombers were capable of pinpoint accuracy against Republican positions and demoralizing terror bombing, typified by the destruction of Guernica. For Hitler, the intervention in Spain served many purposes. First, it allowed for the battle-testing of new military technology and the perfecting of tactics against an enemy equipped and trained by one of Germany's likely enemies in the future – the USSR. Germany's armed forces learnt from the Spanish Civil War important lessons that would aid them in the blitzkriegs of 1939–41, and in this sense the rotation of units in Spain was essential. Second, Republican Spain might come to the aid of France in the case of a German invasion, while a communist-controlled Spain might damage the possibilities of Hitler's intended final reckoning with the USSR. Third, the Condor Legion's services allowed Germany to gain access to Spain's mineral wealth, essential for the expansion of the German military envisaged by Hitler. On 31 October 1936 a contract was established between Germany and the Nationalist authorities by which Germany was to receive 840,000 tons of ore from Morocco. The next round of significant concessions was obtained in July 1937, when the Junta Técnica del Estado agreed to pay Spain's war debt in Reichsmarks, at an annual interest rate of 4 per cent, and to send raw materials to Germany as a guarantee of later payment. Germany was also assured of first option on contracts for the future reconstruction of Spain. Further concessions were extracted in October 1938 when Franco was preparing for the final push on the Ebro front: German firms were finally allowed to acquire substantial control of Spanish mining enterprises, including stakes of up to 100 per cent in companies that operated in Morocco. British concern over the extent of German influence in the Spanish economy in the likely case of a Nationalist victory led to the sending of a diplomatic agent to Burgos on 22 October 1937 – a sure sign that diplomatic recognition would follow if further military successes came Franco's way.

Fourth, Hitler realized that the longer the Spanish Civil War continued, the greater the paralysis of French and British diplomacy would be. By spreading division in France and Great Britain, the war in Spain would prevent these countries from standing up to a still relatively weak Germany as it sought to further its real goals in central Europe, annexing Austria and Czechoslovakia. Finally, complicity with Italy ensured that the latter drifted increasingly into the German orbit. Mussolini needed German cover in order to further his aims in the Mediterranean, fearing, as he did, provoking France and Britain at the same time. German support had a price – becoming a satellite of Germany – which Mussolini was forced to pay. Germany also profited in one unexpected way from the war in Spain. The USSR, disgusted by British and French attitudes to the Axis powers, decided to make a direct arrangement with Hitler, facilitating his conquest of Poland in 1939 and allowing him to turn westwards the following year without fear of a war on two fronts. Dependence on foreign aid was occasionally a source of worry for Franco. He was angry at the Italians' arrogance after being the first to enter Malaga in February 1937, which, despite the lack of real resistance, led them to believe that the rest of the war would be equally simple. Criticism from Italian officers would remain a feature of the war, but Franco tended to ignore it. In 1938, during the Czechoslovakian crisis, a more serious threat arose: German aid came to a halt, and until the crisis was resolved Franco feared being dragged into a generalized European war. This was, however, a minor drawback in the predominantly beneficial relationship with Germany.

German and Italian aid also played a crucial role in financing Franco's war effort. Fundraising was a central concern for the Nationalists, who liked to present themselves to foreign opinion as underdogs whose effort was kept alive by popular contributions. General Mola told *The Times* on 21 October 1936 that 'the people have given all they have to the cause', but in reality the Nationalists had powerful sponsors. Paying for an unexpected war was a problem that Franco had to overcome. He did so through a combination of foreign aid and loans, and, domestically, voluntary fundraising and increased taxation. Foreign help, especially from Germany, was essential in this undertaking. Germany created two holding companies, the Compañía Hispano-Marroquí de Transportes (HISMA), set up in Spain in September 1936, and the Rohstoff-und-Waren Kompensation Handelsgesellschaft (ROWAK), based in Germany, to facilitate the trade between the two countries, which had to be conducted in the form of barter. Exports from the mines of Andalusia, Morocco and, later, Asturias, as well as agricultural products – sherry, olives and wheat – were thus of great importance for Franco. Another important source of support for Franco came from the Texas Oil Company, which agreed to provide him with oil on credit, believing firmly that he would win the war. Italy provided arms in a more generous fashion than Germany, much of her aid being free. Mussolini, having entered the war for reasons of prestige, could not appear to be immediately concerned with repayment. The Nationalists' financial situation improved with every region of Spain that was captured, and the fall of the Basque Country was of crucial importance in this regard. Shipyards, steel plants, munitions and weapons factories had been left intact by the retreating Basques, who could not bring themselves to carry out a scorched-earth policy. The same was to prove true of the Asturians and their mines: future employment prospects were placed above the Republic's strategic interests. By 1938 Basque and Asturian production had risen above pre-war levels, allowing Franco to supply his army's growing needs and to export the remaining mineral products to Germany and Great Britain.

Other countries and individuals helped the Nationalist war effort. Among these, Portugal was the most significant. António Oliveira Salazar, dictatorial prime minister of Portugal since 1932, had always enjoyed tense relations with the Spanish Republic, which harboured Portuguese dissidents and provided a source of inspiration for opposition forces in Portugal. Salazar looked to the Nationalists for a new arrangement which might lead to greater stability in the Iberian peninsula, and from the very first moments aided the insurgents. In the early months of the war, for example, Portugal served as an important corridor uniting the two parts of Nationalist-held territory, allowing for safe communications and the transfer of men and *matériel*. Other favours would follow: ships carrying foreign supplies for the Nationalists were allowed to dock and unload in Portuguese harbours; Republicans who sought to flee from the advancing Nationalist armies by entering Portuguese territory were arrested and returned to the border; the Portuguese press and radio, state-controlled and censored, became useful vehicles for Franco's propaganda, legitimizing, through repetition, Nationalist reports and in the early days of the war keeping up the morale of isolated rebel garrisons. Portugal, lastly, played an important diplomatic role, helping to convince London that Franco intended to replicate Salazar's New State, not Mussolini's Fascist experiment, and slowing down proceedings in the Non-Intervention Committee in London. On 4 October 1936, for example, Portugal indignantly withdrew from the Committee when the USSR suggested that the Portuguese–Spanish border be supervised. Such a scheme was eventually implemented, with supervision of all of Spain's borders and territorial waters being carried out by an international force, but Portugal withdrew its support from the scheme when Germany and Italy pulled their naval forces out of the Mediterranean after a series of aerial attacks in 1937.

There was also important popular support for Franco's cause in Ireland. General Eoin O'Duffy, the most significant figure on the Irish right, sailed for Spain with 700 volunteers only to be returned to Ireland by a disappointed Franco, tired of O'Duffy's posturing and the incompetence of his troops. Moreover, a mass Catholic organization, the Irish Christian Front, was created with the outward purpose of raising funds for medical aid to the Nationalists, although, in reality, it had its own domestic political agenda.

Franco, benefiting from the hesitation of the Western democracies, was able to wage war on the Republic as he wished. His supply of arms was constant; control over Spain's most important agricultural regions ensured a regular supply of foodstuffs for soldiers and civilians alike; and ideologues were busy developing a cult of personality, elevating him to the status of Caudillo, a medieval warrior engaged in a new Reconquista of Spain by purging the country of internal and foreign enemies alike. To dispute Franco's style of leadership became impossible within the Nationalist camp. Even close collaborators such as Juan Yagüe found it prejudicial to speak out. On 19 April 1938 in Burgos Yagüe called for real steps to be taken in the construction of a Falangist state, which required true social reforms to be carried out, and an end to the denigration of the Republic's defenders. These criticisms, motivated by fear of a reactionary dictatorship and a certain war weariness, caused Yagüe to lose the command of the Moroccan corps and led to his house arrest in Burgos for the rest of the year, after which he was reprieved. The warning to Yagüe, like the earlier punishment of Hedilla, was understood and heeded by all.

CHAPTER SIX

Contrasting visions of Spain

Massive political mobilization of the population took place during the Spanish Civil War. Both governments attempted to appeal to all levels of Spanish society and to influence foreign opinion, in the hope of securing ever-greater support, and this chapter outlines the competing visions of Spanish society and culture publicized during the war by Nationalists and different forces within the Republican camp. The rival campaigns were conducted with the help of experience amassed during the First World War, the Russian Civil War and twenty years of divisive mass politics in Spain and in the rest of Europe. They attracted the intellectual support of churchmen, writers and artists, all eager to add their clout to the violent debate that accompanied – indeed, helped to mould – the Spanish Civil War. Once victory had been secured what would be the role of religion, education, women and intellectuals in society? What further reforms would be carried out, or existing measures abolished, in order to modernize Spain and provide her with political stability? What would happen to Catalonia and the Basque Country, and to their respective languages?

6.1 THE NATIONALIST QUEST FOR EMPIRE

There was no consensus among the rebels of 1936 over what shape the future government of Spain would have, and indeed what economic and social path the reworked Spanish state would take. The constitutional monarchy had been discredited by years of sterile politics, and a military dictatorship under General Primo de Rivera had come and gone, failing to make a lasting impression. The venerable debate between strict preservers of privilege and actual reformers, who understood that all sides had to contribute towards the modernization of the country, was alive within the Nationalist coalition. What was surprising was that under conditions as adverse as these Franco's ideologues were able to create a programme for action, even if it was far removed from the realm of the possible. The vision of Spain heralded by Franco's propaganda machine represented a romantic return to a Golden Age that had never existed, and which resulted from a very selective and nationalistic reading of the country's history. The intellectuals at Franco's service proposed to recreate, in the twentieth century, Spain's imperial age, the reigns of Ferdinand and Isabella, of Charles V, and of Philip II, which had seen the expulsion of the Moors from Granada and the sudden and massive expansion of Spanish power around the world. By September 1936 this vision, mixed with the air of modernity provided by Falangist trappings, was asserting itself as the army realized that some kind of ideological programme was necessary in order to sustain and renew its effort.

There were obvious difficulties barring the way of this imperial enterprise. First, there was a war to be won; there were, much more importantly, very serious limitations to Spain's ability to recreate any sort of empire. The pacification of the tiny Moroccan protectorate had been difficult and costly while the rest of Africa had already been carved up by Europe's leading colonial powers. The former Spanish colonies in Latin America, even discounting the influence of the USA and the Monroe Doctrine, showed no desire to accept Spanish guidance and leadership over any aspect of their existence. This did not deter Franco's ideologues as they sought to pin down the qualities of a peculiarly Spanish brand of fascism: according to them, the roadblocks that stood in the way of Spanish greatness (however this was to be defined) were essentially internal. They were the result of foreign influences that had undermined Spanish unity and strength. Liberalism had sapped traditional authority and notions of hierarchy; atheism had spread, weakening religious faith and undoing centuries of social mores; Marxism had turned class against class. Alongside these foreign ideologies, regional separatism in Catalonia, the Basque Country and Galicia threatened the geographical unity of the country. In order to restore Spain to her former greatness a return to what were understood to be the values of the fifteenth and sixteenth centuries was deemed essential. In Spain's Golden Age devotion to the state and the Church and a heroic selflessness had allowed, or so it was proclaimed, material difficulties to be overcome, enabling a handful of men to create the world's greatest empire. Even if such a temporal empire could not be assembled again, there still remained a spiritual conception of empire; the Spanish could be an imperial people even if they did not have an empire to rule, their devotion serving as an example to a materialistic and petty world. Conceptions of empire and spiritual greatness had a lot to do with the resolution of an inferiority complex in the face of contemporary rivals and historic predecessors. Trapped by the cultural notion of decline – and of being the products of an inexorable decline – Franco's supporters responded by a leap into the imaginary, affirming that the material means by which others assessed their greatness were inferior to the spiritual greatness which Spaniards had already demonstrated, and could demonstrate again if properly led.

The way to recreate this imperial age was to follow the example of Franco and to obey his commands. Franco, the Caudillo, was, in Nationalist propaganda, the providential instrument for the salvation of Spain. In clear contrast to the anonymous soldier/worker that was usually depicted in Republican propaganda, Nationalist artists and writers focused on the figure of Franco. He was endlessly praised and presented as the new Cid Campeador – Spain's medieval crusading champion – come to rid Spain of her enemies, a man possessing all virtues and no defects. The elaboration of a personality cult in the 1930s was not a difficult or unusual task, and Falangism's existing dedication to the leader was seized upon by Franco to shore up his position, being elevated to a theory of government – the doctrine of Caudillaje. Intellectuals on the right – men like Ernesto Giménez Caballero, Miguel Martínez del Cerro and Manuel Machado – supported the Nationalist cause, and their concerns with empire and Spain's glorious past were naturally given full support by the budding Nationalist regime. Martínez del Cerro wrote, in his 'Song for the Desired Spain',

I want a Spain the same as that Spain
That 200 years ago fell asleep on us . . .
A perfect and generous Spain, compendium
Of constant efforts and supreme conquests.
A Spain, like that one, fruitful and beneficent
And, like her, hated and attacked;

Made from dreams of virtue and from love,
And with the rigour of effort and discipline.

(Kenwood 1993: 89–90)

The most significant figure in the attempt to provide the Nationalist cause with an intellectual underpinning was José María Pemán, a conservative supporter of the Primo de Rivera dictatorship and a member of parliament during the Republic. Pemán saw the war as a classic tale of good versus evil, or spirit and matter. His concerns can be seen in the title of his most famous wartime work, 'Poem of the Beast and the Angel'. Pemán was eager to turn his views of the war into official orthodoxy, and was allowed to do so in 1939 when he published a history primer for children in which the Civil War was presented as the latest event in a long struggle between Spain and 'anti-Spain': the wars of the Reconquista, the fight against the Protestant Reformation and victory over the Turks at Lepanto.

Education, not surprisingly, was the scene of an important purge. Teachers sympathetic to Popular Front parties were systematically driven away from the profession in order to facilitate the transmission of the new values to the younger generations. A decree issued on 10 December 1936 ensured that the teaching profession would be restricted to those in agreement with the Nationalist cause. Considering the history of education in Spain, this meant opening the doors again to Catholic education. José Permartín Sanjuán, head of the National Secondary and Tertiary Education Service, wrote in 1938 that all of Franco's efforts would be wasted if teachers could not mould the souls of their students, inculcating in them values allegedly undermined by the Second Republic: duty, patriotism and 'a militant religiosity, which constitutes the authentic being of Spain' (Permartín Sanjuán 1938: 6).

During the war, the bulk of the population was kept informed of the developing Nationalist orthodoxy by the Church's unwavering support, by the heavily censored press and, for a time, by General Queipo de Llano's outrageous broadcasts from Seville. These lasted until 1938 with Queipo delivering personal and crude attacks against Republican leaders, soldiers, supporters and women. The press was tightly controlled, the state having given itself the right to determine the number of newspapers and periodicals published, to establish the rules of conduct for journalists and to coordinate their action in order to ensure a unity of message on political and military matters. From

1938 onwards a Falangist takeover of the state propaganda machine was carried out under the supervision of the interior minister, Serrano Suñer, always with the aim of reinforcing Franco's authority.

6.2 THE NATIONAL REVOLUTION

Rebuilding an imaginary empire was hardly a programme, but Franco ultimately depended less on propaganda than his opponents. His stance as a defender of the Church and of property, and the guarantee of immediate purchase of wheat at a high price which his government decreed, earned him the support of millions in rural areas frightened by anticlerical extremism and the prospect of collectivization. The creation of a National Wheat Service symbolized this commitment to the rural world. As one historian puts it, 'the cause was being defended essentially by the peasantry of Old Castile, León, Galicia and Navarre; it was they (and in particular the latter two regions) which provided the shock forces of the nationalist army' (Fraser 1994: 283). The primacy of military power in the Nationalist zone was complete. The army demanded military service of the men in the areas it controlled, and subjected those areas to martial rule. Disobedience of the army's commands, a refusal to fight in its ranks and attempted economic sabotage, or even efforts to secure better wages and working conditions, might be punishable by death. In other words, Franco did not have to convince ordinary people to fight or work for him. Some programmatic larger picture was still necessary, however, not so much to convince men to fight for the Nationalists but rather to mask the differences that existed among them. Notions of empire were not for common consumption; they were destined to make the country's elite feel good about itself in the face of centuries of decline. They also contained the possibility of transforming what was essentially a war for the defence of privilege into a moral struggle for the reassertion of the values that, allegedly, had once made Spain great: the war itself was a means by which to instil these values into a patriotic youth. The attainment of victory required a mixture of qualities identified as being quintessentially Spanish: patriotism, faith, selflessness, obedience and heroism. These values, it was claimed, would not be lost after the war's end, but would instead be used in order to create a united, great and free Spain.

Franco's vision of a traditional and conservative Spain drastically reduced the opportunities which the Republic had begun to open up for women. Nationalist Spain reserved for women the essentially passive role of family orientated guardians of morality. Nevertheless, women were assigned a special – if secondary – place in the Nationalist war effort, because every woman working in the rear areas released a man for the front. The Falangist organization Winter Aid, which developed into Auxilio Social, led by José Antonio's sister Pilar Primo de Rivera, worked as a charity agency distributing food, clothing and medicine to orphans, the aged and the people of newly liberated towns. The Carlist Margaritas provided medical care and support to the troops at the front. On 7 October 1937 all fit and idle women from seventeen to thirty-five were obliged to perform some kind of social service for a minimum of six months; failure to do so would result in the impossibility of securing, in the future, educational qualifications or employment in state-run bodies. Women could, in exceptional times such as the war, work and provide assistance; but it was understood that once the war was over they would return to the domestic sphere – and the Civil War would result in a dramatic step backwards in the status of women in Spain. No special mercy was shown on account of their sex to Republican women, who were deemed to have failed their calling by rearing a generation of revolutionaries and participating in their heinous crimes. After the war there would be no pensions for Republican widows, while divorces granted under the Republic were not recognized by the Francoist state, leading to exceptionally difficult personal situations in the aftermath of the war. Concerns with morality, the status of women and austerity, reflected in frequent press articles regarding the need for all young men to be at the front and demanding the end of idleness in the rear, were, however, always subordinated to the needs of the army. This can be seen by the lack of attempts to curb prostitution: brothels, which continued to exist, were regularly supervised by the authorities for health and security reasons.

In March 1938 the Nationalist government, under Italian pressure, unveiled a piece of legislation which it claimed signalled the arrival of the new Spain. This was the Labour Charter, essentially a reproduction of its Italian Fascist equivalent despite claims to be recreating a Catholic and humanitarian spirit allegedly characteristic of Golden Age Spain. The Charter was meant to demonstrate to Spanish workers that their interests would be looked after by the Falangist state. It guaranteed social insurance, a minimum wage and paid holidays. Peasants were to be allowed a plot of land on which to grow enough food for their families, while tenant farmers were to be protected from expulsion. The Falangist state began to take shape with the Charter through the commitment to the creation of vertical syndicates, which represented both workers and employers. These syndicates were to be gathered in a series of assemblies representing agriculture, shipping, industry and commerce, public and national service, and culture, all of which came together to form the National Corporative Assembly. These syndicates would be guided in their action by three principles: unity, totality and hierarchy. This was the motto developed to replace the Republic's 'liberty, equality and fraternity'. Like all elements of the Falange's programme, however, the Charter was only of tactical value for Franco, its basic provisions regarding land and social benefits being ignored in subsequent years. Powerless within their own party, the old Falangists continued to hope that some time in the future the national-syndicalist revolution might take place; it never did.

It is impossible to overestimate the importance of the Church's role in providing Franco with political legitimacy and in securing the domestic and foreign support he needed in order to prosecute the war successfully. Franco never spoke of a civil war: what was taking place in Spain was a crusade against a foreign enemy, a spiritual conflict both to rid Spain of foreigners and their corrupting ideals and to uphold the primacy of the Catholic Church in Spain's social arrangements. Just as medieval popes had issued bulls for the prosecution of holy wars against Islam, so too did the Spanish Church weigh in behind the Nationalists, recognizing the principles of the crusade, and participating willingly in the search for empire. Cardinal Gomá organized a collective pastoral letter, addressed to the bishops of the whole world. Forty-eight of Spain's most prominent churchmen signed this five-part document which, in an unquestioning manner, affirmed the legitimacy of the Nationalist cause. The rising was described as an intervention to prevent the success of a Soviet plot in Spain and foreign audiences were asked to look upon the executions carried out by the Nationalists as a chance for communists and others to reconcile themselves with God in this lifetime. The Church campaigned for Franco domestically and abroad, the Papacy recognizing Franco's government in May 1938. Its leaders always present at official ceremonies, the Church helped to cement the sometimes precarious coalition aligned behind Franco; it also allowed the Nationalists to reach a mass audience and to establish a link between different social groups, united only through their Catholicism. In return for these services, the Church's social teachings were given the force of law, and it was allowed a much more important role in areas such as education than even the Falange. Later, in 1971, the Spanish Church, in the shape of an assembly of bishops and priests, would criticize its support for, and participation in, the Francoist state that emerged from the war. At that meeting, moreover, a proposal to ask the Spanish people for forgiveness for the Church's role in wartime, when it failed to promote reconciliation at a time of fratricidal fighting, was only narrowly defeated. During the war, however, and in the wake of the unprecedented massacre of religious figures in the Republican area, the Church's attitude was easy to understand; only a Nationalist victory seemed to ensure the continued existence of the Church on Spanish soil.

Catholic teaching provided much of the language and the concepts that were central to Nationalist propaganda. The crusade was portrayed as a demonstration of self-sacrifice, a process by which the individual and indeed Spain herself could expiate sins in the search for purification. The need for violence, however, was not explained purely in religious terms. Race theory and eugenics were introduced into the Spanish equation by figures such as Antonio Vallejo Nágera, Professor of Psychiatry in Madrid, who argued that the Spanish race had to be protected both from foreign influences and weaker 'racial strains', and that this need had long been understood in Spain, having been present in the early modern concept of purity of the blood. Interpreted in this light, the rising was a last-ditch attempt to save the Spanish race from corruption. This confusion between political beliefs and medical matters contributed to the portrayal of the Republicans as diseased individuals who, for the good of Spain, had to be eliminated; Marxism and other revolutionary doctrines were presented regularly as infectious diseases threatening Spain.

It was also through the Catholic Church, and Catholic associations and individuals, that Franco's case abroad was made most effectively. The Nationalist position, as presented to the rest of the world, was simple. Franco and his fellow officers had risen to prevent an imminent communist bid for power. The Popular Front government was not legitimate because of both the violent conditions in which the 1936 elections were held and its actions since February of that year. The members of the Popular Front did not hold a moral high ground because they too had attempted to overthrow the legitimate government of the Republic in 1934. By endlessly repeating these simple statements, and by drawing the world's attention to the atrocities committed by the 'Reds' in 1936, the Nationalists and their supporters reinforced the political will not to intervene in Spain prevalent in the chanceries of the democratic nations. V.A. Cazalet MP, for example, wrote to *The Times* on 4 February 1937 detailing 'Red' atrocities and stating that 'the reign of terror still continues unabated in the Red territory'; Major General J.F.C. Fuller, in his *The Conquest of Red Spain*, stated that the Republicans had 'capitulated to the rabble. Arms were handed out to the denizens of the world, and the "East Ends" of the cities went roaring red' (Fuller 1937: 10). The Church's involvement in the foreign propaganda campaign helped to reinforce the idea that Franco was an outright defender of traditional values rather than a Spanish Mussolini. The officers' rising in 1936 might have been unpalatable, but so too seemed to be the alternative; in such conditions non-intervention (intrinsically favourable, as we have seen, to Franco) seemed to be the most sensible option. The Nationalists did not have to convince public opinion in the democratic nations to come to their aid, but, rather, not to help the Republic. Theirs was an easy task. Quality was not essential; Arthur Koestler, who participated in the Republic's propaganda offensive, claimed that the offerings of the rival campaign looked as if they had been 'concocted by illiterates', but he was missing the point. The increasing importance of Soviet aid for the Republican war effort facilitated Franco's propaganda. Pro-Nationalist propaganda was simplistic and virulent; all the pro-Republican factions, from Azaña's followers to the FAI, were lumped together as 'Red' and held to be both responsible for the atrocities of the summer of 1936 and working in accordance with a plan dictated from Moscow. Arnold Lunn wrote, in his pamphlet *The Unpopular Front*, one of the many propaganda pieces published by the London firm Burns, Oates & Washbourne, 'the Red Death, which is spreading like a plague over modern Europe, is far more devastating in its effects than the Black Death of the fourteenth century, and we are fighting it with methods compared with which medieval therapeutics were scientific' (Lunn 1937: 19). Pro-Republican commentators presented evidence against such a simplification, but it kept reappearing until the end of the war.

In Germany, Italy and Portugal, Franco's principal foreign sources of support, political conditions made an open discussion of events in Spain impossible. A friendly country was being saved from a communist plot; this line was repeated without any possible contradiction. Intervention in the Spanish emergency was used to shore up domestic support for the Fascist and National Socialist regimes. For Joseph Goebbels, Franco was demonstrating the power of the individual will and waging a fight for civilization against a plot organized in, and run from, Moscow. The support for the Republic found in the Western democracies resulted from the ideological root shared by democracy and communism – 'a morbid humanitarian liberalism' – which made them the 'same form of mental disease' (Goebbels 1937: 10). Lastly, Bolshevism was essentially a cover for Jewish activities against Western civilization, including such basic elements as the family, threatened by the 'socialization of women'. According to Goebbels, Jewish organizations were supplying the Republic with the weapons it needed to prosecute the war successfully. The ultimate aim of this Jewish plot was to lead the nations of Europe to war against each other, fatally weakening them (Goebbels 1937). No accusation was too low for the Nazi propaganda machine, which went as far as to claim that Republican soldiers were being issued with 'rape vouchers' as a form of payment for their services. Technical and professional contributions to the Nationalist propaganda campaign were also made by Franco's foreign allies. Forty films would be produced in Nationalist Spain despite the difficulties caused by the Republican government's control of Barcelona and Madrid, where the country's main studios were located; others would be produced in countries friendly to Franco. Films were also processed and printed in Portuguese, Italian and German studios, and Germany offered technicians and material to the Nationalist film industry.

6.3 THE REAFFIRMATION OF REPUBLICAN VALUES

Political mobilization was of greater importance and difficulty for the Republic. Its leadership did not, in the first months of the conflict, have the power and the will to force men and women to fight and work for the regime. The Republic, and the organizations that fought in its name, had to convince people of the justice of their cause. Abroad, the same approach was followed by Republican propaganda: help from the Western democracies would only arrive if public opinion became convinced of the need to help the Spanish Republic survive. The near collapse of the Republic in the summer of 1936 makes it difficult to talk about Republican political mobilization in the early part of the conflict, because the true engines of that mobilization were beyond the control of the state. Moreover, the idealized picture of the future Spain which was being built through the sacrifice of war varied enormously. The CNT's vision was truly revolutionary: in a Spain with no state, no government, no army or police and no money, collectives, town councils and unions would deal with each other directly, complementing their abilities and resources. To many in the UGT this vision of a union-run country was dazzling, but to everyone else it was an impractical and dangerous utopia. The POUM also called for a revolution, albeit one that would establish a dictatorship of the proletariat in order to wage the war against Franco more efficiently. The other political parties, slower to operate in the new context, also became active in the attempt to convince men and women to cooperate in the war effort: not the republicans, whose parties disintegrated in the wake of the coup and the revolution that followed, but rather the socialists and the communists, the mainstays of the regime until 1939. The PSOE, and especially the PCE, promised the establishment of a new Republic that, preserving its parliamentary nature, would be free from the influence of the reactionary elements who had prevented social reforms from taking place from 1931 to 1936.

Revolution and government-led political mobilization were in many ways incompatible. In order to prosecute the war more effectively, the Republican government felt that it must centralize authority in itself, away from regional governments, local councils and the unions, while at the same time maximizing industrial and agricultural production. Curbing the power of the CNT and other revolutionary organizations had the added benefit of helping to convince foreign opinion of the Republic's legitimacy and ability to enforce the rule of law. All of these objectives clashed directly with the ambitions of many who saw the war as an opportunity to further their political and social aims. Rationalization of industrial production could not be reconciled with workers' power as expressed in the collectivized factories of Barcelona. An increased agricultural output to make up for the loss of Spain's principal agricultural regions could not be reconciled with collectivized farms. Anarcho-syndicalists had achieved many of their goals within the first weeks of the war.

For them, campaigns of political mobilization to strengthen the regime were a source of danger and, ultimately, of disappointment. No republic could ever deliver what the people in arms had provided for themselves in July 1936. In other words, what Republican governments presented as reforms invariably involved a defeat for the CNT. The same could be said for regionalist politicians in Catalonia, for whom the Republic's increased strength from 1937 onwards spelt the end of a glorious period of almost complete independence, and also for the POUM.

Political mobilization by the Popular Front governments had thus a number of objectives: preparing the population for war; reintegrating it into the Republican whole by demonstrating the strength and legitimacy of the regime; and outlining the vision of a post-victory Republic which, free from reactionary influences, could deliver a better life for workers and peasants. All of this was to be achieved while the right to property and the preservation of parliamentary democracy were assured. Hampered by the hostility of revolutionaries to the Second Republic, the Popular Front was further undermined by the international attitude to its plight, always hard to explain to the population, and by the steady reversals on the military front. The defence of Madrid, combined with tales of atrocities (made especially gruesome when they involved Franco's Moorish troops, accused of savage cruelty and of being motivated above all by sexual desire), could not serve indefinitely as the backbone of propaganda. A successful offensive was necessary to demonstrate that the Republic could ultimately survive the ordeal of war. No such offensive was forthcoming, however, and Republican propaganda lost its effectiveness. Too many times a decisive breakthrough was prematurely and wrongly announced. In May 1938, in the aftermath of the Nationalists' breakthrough to the Mediterranean, Negrín launched an important propaganda campaign, defining the Thirteen Points for which the Republic was fighting. These Thirteen Points aimed essentially to keep Spain politically and economically independent, with a politically neutral army to defend it, and to preserve personal liberties (including liberty of conscience and the right to property, the latter nevertheless conditioned, as had been the case since 1931, by agrarian reform). The Thirteen Points allowed the Republic itself to be called into question because the programme envisaged a direct consultation of the Spanish people on the nature of regime under which they preferred to live. Defining war aims so explicitly was important for internal morale purposes. It also presented a description of what it would take to bring the fighting to an end, thus signifying, internationally, a willingness to negotiate and appear reasonable. The clearest vision of the future of the Republic, and the importance of the struggle, was made precisely in 1938, in a series of pamphlets entitled *Charlas populares: Lo que significa la guerra* (*Popular chats: the meaning of the war*). A pamphlet was issued by each ministry, establishing a comparison between life in the two zones into which Spain had been divided since July 1936, and between life under the Republic and the monarchy (with which the Nationalist cause was associated throughout the series). Thus, the Ministry of Agriculture concentrated its attention on the life of peasants in the Nationalist zone. Deprived of syndical associations through which to defend themselves, peasants were at the mercy of landowners, *caciques* and the Guardia Civil; land redistribution had been overturned and the daily pay was meagre. Having illustrated the state of affairs in the Nationalist zone, and compared it to life in the Republican zone, where agrarian reform was well under way, the Ministry of Agriculture then spelt out the duties of Republican peasants. These included an increase in production to meet both the needs of the fighting men at the front and the foreign currency needs of the government; the replacement of middlemen and other speculators by cooperative ventures (not the same as collectives) capable of selling directly to the consumers; and covering the shortfall created by the incorporation of peasants in the Popular Army without complaint about the extra hours involved.

The same approach was followed by other ministries. The Ministry of National Defence praised the creation of the Popular Army, and the individual soldiers who constituted it. Here were men who fought for the values of dignity, liberty, law, social justice, democracy, humanity and Spanish independence – 'for the new and authentic Spain, which wants, but has hitherto never been allowed, to exist' – and against class privilege, ambition, treason and mindless imitation of foreign dictatorial systems. The Foreign Ministry insisted on the international character of the war against the Republic, stating that Hitler, Mussolini and Salazar were seeking out raw materials and strategic advantages in Spain. It also outlined both the diplomatic struggle of the Republic, which was having 'magnificent results', and the future diplomacy of Spain, built upon the principles of peace, liberty and solidarity among the democracies. The Ministry of the

Interior compared the maintenance of law and order in both zones. In the Republican zone overt and covert activities to preserve peace and help win the war were carried out with full legality and responsibility; in the Nationalist zone, however, the population was cowed by the systematic use of terror, including the rape of Spanish women by Moorish troops. The Ministry of Finance and the Economy drew a parallel between the economic life of Spain under the monarchy – controlled by a narrow class whose members sat on numerous management boards and were dependent on foreign capital – and that of the Nationalist zone, where nothing had changed. There was no popular control of economic matters, foreigners laid claim to Spain's most important resources, and the bulk of the population was burdened by a heavy fiscal load. Against this pattern stood the economic life of the Republic, where the economy had been placed at the service of the people. The property of those who sided with the rebels was now in public hands, and thanks to the proper administration of public funds the ingrained notion of Spain's poverty was being dispelled. An army had been created and equipped, soldiers' families were receiving pensions, medical care was being provided on a greater scale than before and another massive effort was being made in the field of education. According to a pamphlet issued by the Ministry of Finance, the future of the Republic was to be a prosperous one: 'No longer will there be peasants without land and unproductive lands, only fecund and joyous fields. The number of factories will multiply and the mines will overflow with their wealth. The Spanish people will know how to direct, towards their well-being and aggrandizement, the immense resources which the mother country contains.'

The Ministry of Education and Health stated that the Republic stood for the popularization of culture, now open to all rather than the elite. The Republic's work in the field of education had not been halted by the war; whereas in 1935 a million pesetas had been spent in the construction of new schools, in 1937, despite the war, 64 million pesetas were spent for the same purpose. Volunteer organizations were carrying on the fight against adult illiteracy, and it was as a result of this massive national effort, according to the Ministry, that the people were now defending the Republic, being 'willing to make all the necessary sacrifices' to save it from internal and foreign foes. The Ministry of Justice took the same road as that of Finance, pointing out that the same vices to be found in the administration of justice under the monarchy were to be found now

111

in the Nationalist zone. Privilege ruled supreme; there was no rule of law and no respect for the rights of citizens. In the case of the Republic, however, and since the start of the war, profound changes had taken place in the judicial system, which now, with the popular tribunals, had the people at its heart. The series of pamphlets was anchored by that issued by the Presidency of the Council of Ministers, which attempted to give the meaning of the war according to Prime Minister Juan Negrín. Resorting to traditional patriotic images of Spain, the pamphlet presented the conflict as a national war of independence against German and Italian fascists aided by domestic traitors – generals, landowners and capitalists – who were united only by their greed and hatred of the people, and who had offered their support for the foreign dictators at private meetings throughout the decade. The strength of the contacts and the detailed nature of these treacherous plans were reflected by the speed with which foreign armaments reached Spain. Moreover, the German and Italian press were completely open about the fact that their troops had invaded Spain, and that the plunder of Spain's economic resources had begun. These plans would fail, however, thwarted by a people defending its dignity. The Republic's government had united the efforts of all for the attainment of victory, and the Popular Army was a reflection of this new will. Life in the rearguard was being organized to ensure a peaceful increase in production, while all Spaniards were finally united by a common desire to defeat the enemy.

This, then, was the view of the war as presented by the Spanish Republic's government in 1938. Revolutionary tendencies were played down, and the Republic was pledged to the defence of other European democracies from fascist attack; little or no mention was made of the divisive regional question in Spain. This was the message of a centralizing government which commanded an increasingly effective army and which was able to impose its will in the rearguard. In the pamphlets history was being rewritten at a furious pace in order to minimize the achievements of the revolutionary months that followed the rising of July 1936. Order, it was now said, had been maintained by the Republic from the start, and changes made by the Republic's apparatus in order to survive the new circumstances – such as the popular tribunals – were presented as logical and planned reforms. It had taken the Republic a long time to put forward such a coherent propaganda message, and in many ways it was already too late. By 1938 its chances of military victory were slim.

6.4 SELF-MOBILIZATION IN THE REPUBLICAN ZONE

Forces opposed to the Nationalists, controlling as they did the main centres of population in Spain, and the main printing and artistic centres, had been able to mount an important, if incoherent, propaganda offensive from late 1936 onwards. Parties and unions had their own newspapers, to which were added new titles following the seizure of conservative newspaper offices in the loyal cities. The print media, unlike in the Nationalist zone, was allowed to present differing viewpoints to its audience, although censorship on military matters eventually developed. In an atmosphere of revolution and war against conservative interests, the range of opinions that found their way into press was naturally restricted. One union heavily involved in this effort was the Federación Española de Trabajadores de la Enseñanza (FETE – Spanish Federation of Education Workers). Like many unions, the FETE formed a militia battalion which was active on the Madrid front from November 1936 onwards; at the same time it dedicated itself to the struggle against illiteracy, female members serving as 'hospital readers' and organizing colonies for refugee children in the rear. It was not just these socialist teachers who were concerned with education; it remained, even in wartime, a priority for the Republic, a central part of its mission of enlightenment. One thousand new schools, it was claimed, were opened in 1937, despite pressing concerns on the battlefield. The reasons for this were simple, and went beyond the immediate – and real – devotion to education: in wartime each school became a centre for official propaganda aimed at children and, through them, the adult population. The idea of culture as a liberating force was one of the Republic's most powerful rhetorical weapons, allowing as it did the possibility of self-improvement without recourse to the violent or revolutionary activity preached by anarchists.

Similar to the commitment shown by the Republic to education, because it was linked to the notion of liberation, was the regime's wartime stance towards women. Until 1936 the Republic had made an attempt to improve women's social standing through legislation, trying to ensure that men and women became at least legally equal. Women had been allowed to vote for the first time in 1933, while the possibility of divorce had been made available by the regime. Now, as women were needed in the war effort in order to release men for the front, the policy was continued and strengthened by government and private associations alike. The anarchists were most radical in this respect, encouraging a change in the overall attitude towards women and sexuality; Federica Montseny, as health minister, opened a series of medical centres for women and legalized abortion. In some cases women in the popular militias participated in the fighting in the early months of the war. This practice was, however, quickly reined in by the Republican government because of doubts over women's effectiveness at the front and the poor impression that women soldiers made abroad. Nevertheless, the importance attributed to women as economic producers was undeniable, as was the responsibility handed to them for the first time, even if not all men were ready to accept the government's efforts in this field.

A distinctive feature of the Republic's war was the commitment shown by artists and intellectuals who perceived it as their duty to contribute to the war effort through their work, presented in such a way as to be understood and appreciated by as wide an audience as possible. Successive intellectuals' manifestos made this support clear, even if some of the early signatories preferred to leave Spain quietly and quickly. The murder of the poet and playwright Federico García Lorca in the very first days of the war by Nationalist forces galvanized Spanish intellectuals, who identified the Nationalists as enemies of culture. The avant-garde spirit of the 1920s was dropped in favour of traditional forms of literature and art in order to stimulate the civilian population and the soldiers to endure further sacrifices in the search for victory. This led to a high value being placed on popular literary production (especially the writing of ballads, already explored before the war by García Lorca and Antonio Machado), esteemed to be not only a measure of the Spanish genius, but of the Republic's mission to nourish that genius. Every poem published by a soldier or a worker was presented as a spiritual victory for the Republic, which was freeing its people from centuries of ignorance. Perhaps the most important figure in the literary effort in support of the Republic was Antonio Machado (whose brother Manuel performed a similar task for the Nationalists), who would die in exile shortly after the war's end. Reviews such as *El mono azul* and *Hora de España* showed a great desire to bring together established writers such as Machado and the unheard voices in the ranks of the militias. Over fifty anthologies of war ballads were published during the conflict, and popular reviews published over 8,500 poems.

This need to intervene in the war through their writings and their art was felt not only by Spanish intellectuals and artists but by their counterparts all over the world. Intellectuals, increasingly troubled by the rise of fascism, became convinced that the time had come for them to declare their political allegiance and offer their services for a concrete political cause. These writers portrayed the war as a popular struggle against oppressive privilege, as the birth-pangs of a better world. The Chilean poet Pablo Neruda described the enemies of the Republic in the following manner:

Bandits with planes and with Moors
Bandits with rings and duchesses
Bandits with black friars spitting out blessings
(Kenwood 1993: 132–3)

Battle was joined not only in the trenches but in newspaper columns, pamphlets and art galleries, in a clear attempt to make up for the two-faced policy of non-intervention which British, French and American writers saw as a terrible embarrassment. The supreme example of these intellectual concerns was the Second International Writers' Congress for the Defence of Culture, held in Spain in 1937. Writers from all over the world attended the sessions in Barcelona, Valencia and Madrid. The topics debated included humanism, the problems of Spanish culture, the role of the artist in society and the reinforcement of international cultural links. The main conclusion reached was that art could not be dissociated from political commitments, and that it had to be accessible to the people. Whatever the quality of the arguments, and despite the almost inevitable political divisions that emerged during the Congress, the message of solidarity for Spanish intellectuals and the Republican war effort in general was potent. Foreign writers and poets assisted in fundraising activities for the Republic's cause, and flocked to Spain as journalists, ambulance drivers and soldiers. The French writer André Malraux went further, organizing a mercenary air squadron, complete with aeroplanes, and publishing in 1937 *L'Espoir*, a propaganda work disguised as a novel, which essentially endorsed the communist position in Spain. Few at the time realized that their unquestioning support for the Republican side, as expressed through international links maintained primarily by the communist parties of Europe, was potentially harming the future of democracy in Spain. George Orwell, who fought in Spain not with the International Brigades but with the POUM's militia, was lucky to leave Spain alive once the attack on the POUM began, and his *Homage to Catalonia* is a powerful reminder of the scale of the rivalries and tensions within the Republican camp, by no means a haven of pluralism.

Artistic production was also mixed with the need to educate recruits to the Popular Army about the reasons why the war was being fought. Theatre played an important role, its ability to reach large audiences with a cultural and political message having been recognized in the Second Republic by artists such as García Lorca. Theatre was deemed to stiffen morale at the front, by turning the social and political questions behind the war into human situations more readily understandable by the soldiers, and the war years saw an explosion in playwriting. Agit-prop companies were active in the front and in the rear, their innovative styles contrasting readily with the Nationalists' reluctance to stage anything other than Golden Age and religious plays. The political education of the soldiers was also one of the tasks entrusted to the commissars of the Popular Army. Posters, seen since the start of the century as a vital tool for the transmission of simple and effective political messages, also became a characteristic of the Republican mobilization effort, being used by parties and unions to stress a range of issues, from the need for union in order to defeat fascism to the need for care in order not to contract venereal diseases. Significant Spanish painters such as Joan Miró and Pablo Picasso were commissioned by the Republican government to provide works for the Spanish pavilion at the International Exhibition in Paris, held in 1937; Picasso's contribution, *Guernica*, is arguably the most famous painting of the twentieth century. Finally, of course, there was cinema, with both full-length fiction films and shorter propaganda newsreels being produced by a number of agencies that controlled the country's studios – the CNT-FAI, the Catalan Generalitat and the PCE. Further films were made in the USSR and France, where André Malraux continued his tireless efforts for the Republic by directing *Sierra de Teruel*.

The Communist Party, through its international connections and its clear desire to strengthen the hand of the state, played a significant role in the Republic's propaganda at home and abroad. Spanish communists could draw on the lessons learnt by the Bolsheviks in the Russian Civil War, and a host of communist-dominated organizations around the world could be relied upon to disseminate the party's interpretation of events in Spain. Thus, in August 1936 a Popular Front delegation headed by the communist deputy Dolores Ibárruri (better known as La Pasionaria) was in Paris. Addressing a large rally in the French capital, La Pasionaria added a number of emblematic slogans to the Republic's lexicon: *'no pasarán'* and 'it is better to die on one's feet than to live on one's knees'. In October 1936 the American League Against War and Fascism published a pamphlet entitled *Spain's Democracy Talks to America* in which a host of Spanish political figures, veterans of the fighting, and even a Catholic priest appealed for help from abroad. As La Pasionaria put it, 'We find it hard to understand how the government of the French Republic, the country of liberty and of the revolution, does not come to the aid of a government regularly elected by the Spanish people . . . Heroism is not enough in this struggle; we need help!' It was the PCE that encouraged the people of Madrid to believe that they could defend their city and that gained most in propaganda terms from the ensuing battle. The PCE's posters covered the city's walls while La Pasionaria harangued its defenders. Communist aid preserved the city; foreign communists, who had been mistaken for Russians on their arrival to Madrid, were fighting and dying in the trenches of the university campus. Another communist propaganda triumph was the elevation of General Miaja to the status of saviour of Madrid. Miaja himself, when handed command of the capital, was convinced that he was being set up by Largo Caballero as a scapegoat for the loss of Madrid. As the city held, however, Miaja became increasingly dependent on the communists, whose units were instrumental to the military triumph, and who convinced him of his own merit and ability while securing positions of power in the Junta he headed. Miaja was a popular hero for no reason other than the people of Madrid's need for a hero and for a simple explanation for their collective victory. The PCE's bid for a monopoly on the propaganda front was facilitated by the reluctance of the Republic's leading figures to become involved. Azaña did not view it as part of his presidential duties, occasionally speaking to the country by radio to highlight the international dimension of the war; Prieto was even more sparing with words, fearing that his pessimism would ring out; and Largo Caballero, after his fall from power, was kept away from the public by the government, his talents being lost to the Republic's cause.

All of these efforts counted for little in the face of mounting hardship and the continued military reversals. In September 1937

Azaña privately blamed the people for purchasing goods on the black market, rather than denouncing illegal sales to the authorities. This was an uncharitable attitude on the part of the president, but the existence of a black market raised many questions about the extent of solidarity among the Republic's nominal supporters. By the winter of 1938–9 the citizens of Madrid, with no fuel to keep themselves warm, were reduced to a diet of lentils (ironically known as 'Dr Negrín's victory pills'), beans, rice and, occasionally, salt cod. Even rations for the troops were declining in the face of irregular supplies from abroad and the disappearance into the black market of much of the harvest. Sugar had disappeared from the shops; it could only be purchased with a medical prescription. Manuel Azcárate, a young communist writer sent to Madrid after the fall of Barcelona to aid the ailing propaganda campaign, realized immediately after his arrival that the fighting spirit of the capital, so much in evidence in 1936, had completely disappeared. The reasons were obvious: 'War weariness was written on the emaciated faces. The mood had become dark, sad and tragic. There was a generalized anti-communist resentment because many believed the communists to be responsible for the war's prolongation' (Azcárate 1994: 158). On its own, cultural dynamism was ultimately incapable of keeping the fighting spirit of Republican soldiers and civilians alive.

Aftermath

By the end of the Spanish Civil War in April 1939 the country was in ruins. Hundreds of thousands died in the fighting or were executed. Executions continued at a hurried pace after the war's end; Galeazzo Ciano, Mussolini's son-in-law and foreign minister, was shocked by what he saw in Spain in the summer of 1939. Over 400,000 people went into exile, and there was an army of wounded to be looked after. When Franco took full control of Spain the country's economy was in a critical state. Three years of civil war had left Spain with an economic output one-third lower than that of 1935; the labour force had lost over half a million men and women. Only two-thirds of the livestock remained, along with half of the railway stock. The country's gold reserves had been spent by the Republic on armaments, while the Nationalists had mortgaged the country's future wealth in their struggle to win the war. The loss to Spain's national life was enormous; those in exile were barred from contributing to the country's recovery and there was no hope in the immediate future of any gesture of reconciliation. Moreover, Franco would continue to work to keep the spirit of his crusade alive.

It was important for Franco to do so because his position, despite success in the war, was essentially precarious. His power was absolute, but it had been conferred on him because of the circumstances of the war, especially the need to achieve a complete military victory. His supporters were not, it must be remembered, necessarily committed to the continuation of his personal rule. Monarchists – and there were many in the upper echelons of the army – saw military victory as the first step on the road to a restoration of the monarchy (although they were of course weakened by conflicting claims to the Spanish throne). Old-style Falangists, on the other hand, saw victory in the context of an increasingly totalitarian Europe, and longed to see their party's doctrine applied without interference from either the army or the Church. These elements within the FET y de las JONS, although isolated, wanted to carry out a national-syndical revolution in Spain, and despaired of the reactionary forces which were content with suppressing all attempted social reforms. Franco had to ride the tensions between the two groups and the only way to do so was to reaffirm constantly the danger that faced them all should he be weakened to any extent. At the same time, Franco constantly sought new ways to explain why power should be concentrated in his hands. His authority, essentially charis-matic during the war, acquired in the 1940s a traditional aspect. Like a monarch, the Caudillo now claimed to rule by the grace of God. By the 1960s Franco's right to rule Spain would be founded upon his ability to maintain peace and deliver economic growth and prosperity.

Franco's position was improved by the rapid outbreak of the Second World War and by the course the conflict took. In the face of the dangers of war, unity and strong leadership were required; it was natural that Franco should remain in his position until the dust had settled in Europe. Franco was to ride the storm success-fully by breaking the war into various component parts. There was Germany's war against the USSR, which he viewed as necessary struggle against communism and to which he contributed the Blue Division. Having been officially organized by the Falange, this unit did not lead to Spain being classified as a belligerent. There was also the war between the Western powers, which Franco described as a calamity, and the war in the Far East, in which he supported the Allies unreservedly. Aware of Spain's military weakness, Franco kept Spain out of the war (Germany having failed to promise sufficient rewards to tempt Franco to enter the conflict), establishing an Iberian pact of friendship with Salazar for common protection. This position allowed him to obtain much-needed materials from the Allies, to supply the Nazi war effort in return for foreign exchange and, on the domestic stage, to carry out whatever cabinet changes would allow him to remain in power.

Even after the Second World War had come to an end, the memory of the Civil War was kept alive by Franco and his close supporters. All those who had participated in the Nationalist war effort were continuously reminded of their responsibility in the events of the war – of their membership, in other words, of the 'pact of blood'. They were in a privileged position because they had won the war; their privileges would come to an end should their views of the war ever waver. To reinforce this sense of a two-tiered nation, no genuine hand of friendship was ever extended to those who had fought on the Republican side. There were no pensions for Republican wounded, widows or orphans; working conditions and salaries in city and country were extremely low; the burdens of taxation and of the black-market economy fell on the poor. The defeated paid the cost of Spain's slow reconstruction, with any attempt at dissent or questioning punished in the most severe of ways. Republican supporters were outcasts in their own country, held up as living examples of what would happen if the Nationalist coalition ever broke down. They were denied the possibility of mourning their war dead, or of publicly articulating their views of what the war had been about. Legal measures enshrined the gulf between winners and losers: purges in the civil service and the teaching profession rewarded Nationalist supporters, while a percentage of public jobs was reserved for Nationalist veterans and wounded. The gulf between the two camps was barely bridged by a series of pardons that followed the Second World War and continued throughout the duration of the Franco regime, celebrating both political and religious milestones. There were so many pardons, in fact, that one might wonder about their practical value. The plight of the defeated was symbolized by the employment of prisoners to rebuild Spain's infrastructure and, more specifically, to build over a period of twenty years the gigantic monument to Franco's victory, the Valle de los Caídos (Valley of the Fallen), outside Madrid. Many would die in this crude attempt to force Republican prisoners to expiate their sins by employment as cheap labour under harsh conditions. Other monuments were planned to commemorate the triumph of the crusade, such as the Victory Arch in Madrid, located in the University City, which represented a clear sign that even in the site of the Republic's greatest victory Francoism had been ultimately triumphant. Curiously, though, the Arch, completed in 1955, was not officially inaugurated, an indication that Franco's regime eventually understood that its triumphal policy was not always well received.

This gradual change of heart can also be followed in the historiography and official descriptions of the conflict. Initial school textbooks like those of José María Pemán – *La historia de España contada con sencillez (The History of Spain Told with Simplicity)* – presented, as we have seen, a Manichaean vision of the Spanish Civil War, fought by Spain – good – and anti-Spain – evil. By the 1960s a change had occurred. The state had less control over the media, and alternative views of the conflict were being discussed; the influence of foreign authors was also being felt. A rearguard action was undertaken by the regime in order to continue to shape opinion on the war and continue to be legitimated by it. Ricardo de la Cierva, an official in the Ministry of Information and Tourism, was at the forefront of this attempt to counteract the influence of foreign publications, using for the first time Republican sources, and no longer speaking of the 'crusade' but of the 'Spanish war'. De la Cierva and other likeminded historians claimed to bring scientific methods to the study of the conflict. The new orthodoxy was that blame for the tragedy of war lay with all parts. Intransigence had made violence impossible to avoid; but Franco's rule was legitimated by the Caudillo's ability to bring peace to such a divided country. It was Franco the peacemaker that should be celebrated, and not Franco the warrior.

Why did this change take place? First, there was a clear clash of generations between those who remembered the war, those who grew up in the years of poverty that followed it and those growing up in the increasingly prosperous 1960s. Hatred could not be sustained indefinitely, especially in the context of a country undergoing a radical economic transformation. In 1959 a new economic policy was embarked upon, by which, after a period of stabilization, the Spanish economy was liberalized and opened to foreign influence. A discourse of blame and recrimination had little place in the context of a regime which officially portrayed itself as progressive and modernizing, and which increasingly attributed its right to exist to these qualities. Franco's maintenance of peace had made prosperity possible; calling the regime into question meant jeopardizing improved living standards.

There was, of course, another Spain, beyond that of victors and vanquished coexisting within the country's borders. Over 400,000 men and women had been forced to leave the country in 1939. This was an immense blow to Spain, especially if we consider this mass exile not merely in terms of numbers but of the skills lost to Spain: intellectuals and artists, teachers and professors, leading politicians and professionals. Anyone whose political beliefs had brought him or her to declare for the Republic fled. As if to confirm this, exiled Spain would produce two Nobel Prize-winners – Juan Ramón Jiménez and Severo Ochoa. For the Republican exiles life was difficult. They were broken down into two main groups: those who found their way to Mexico and other Latin American states, and those who remained in France. Mexico, which never recognized the Franco government, remaining loyal to the increasingly fictitious Republic, was the ideal destination; in 1940, for example, Mexico extended Mexican nationality to all exiles who desired to take it up. Exile in France was more tragic. Having been herded by the French authorities into refugee camps upon their arrival, many were still in the camps when France was defeated in 1940. Conditions were poor, and the Vichy authorities were not sympathetic to the plight of leftist exiles. Some, like Lluys Companys, were returned to Spain to be executed; others ended their lives in German concentration camps. Others still joined the French resistance. Mexican exiles had a different background and different worries; they had the luxury of engaging in intellectual pursuits, returning repeatedly to the 'Spanish problem'. They reflected on matters such as exile, Spanish decadence, nostalgia for the homeland, the Spanish Civil War and its place in history, the dictatorship and the meaning of Spanish culture.

Divisions among exiles did not exist merely in geographical terms. All of the frustrations borne of defeat were carried into exile. The communists were despised by other groups, unjustly accused of being responsible for the eventual fate of the Republic. Negrín was also – again unjustly – lumped with the PCE and ostracized. Matters had not been altered in 1950, when the PCE finally decided to abandon the armed struggle against the regime, and in 1956, when the party proposed a strategy of national reconciliation. The rift between Negrín and Prieto, for example, gave rise to a bitter and pointless correspondence between the two men, who were reduced to fighting over the meagre spoils of defeat – the funds which had been salted away in preparation for exile.

As the Second World War came to an end and France was liberated, the exiles' hope of a return to Spain naturally increased. Franco had become an international pariah: he ruled over Spain because of the support he had received in the Civil War – widely seen by late 1944 as a prelude to the Second World War – from Mussolini and Hitler. He had contributed with supplies and volunteers to the German war effort. Spanish exiles hoped that in the post-war world order there would be no place for Franco. Some were not willing to wait until diplomatic action had removed him from power, and a guerrilla campaign started in 1944 from French territory. Its aim was to spark off a popular revolt against Franco; the numbers involved were too few, however, and Franco's hold on Spain was too strong. Five years of his rule had broken the will of surviving Republicans within Spain to resist him. Undeterred, Republicans in exile looked to the Western democracies and the Soviet Union for help, but once again they were disappointed. There were many speeches against Franco; Spain was prevented from joining the United Nations and its various bodies; economic sanctions were imposed; the Marshall Plan was deemed not to apply to Franco; but no concrete steps to remove him from power were made. Moreover, as the post-war climate soured and the Cold War broke out, Franco's anti-communist stance shone brighter than his regime's genealogy. Collaboration with Franco was deemed to be essential for the defence of Western Europe, and slowly all the restrictions imposed upon Spain were lifted; Franco's support came at the price of massive injections of American capital into Spain's severely weakened economy. This period represents in many ways the West's second betrayal of democracy in Spain: having failed to allow the Republic to buy weapons with which to fight, Britain, France and the USA now subordinated concerns for the future of Spain for the purposes of containing communism in Europe. It would take Franco's death and the increasing cooperation between, on the one hand, internal and exiled opposition figures and, on the other, reformers within the Franco regime to plan Spain's peaceful transition to a compromise solution: parliamentary democracy under a restored monarchy.

Chronology

1936

17 July	Military rising begins in Morocco.
18 July	Prime Minister Casares Quiroga resigns.
19 July	Martínez Barrio resigns; Giral named prime minister, orders the distribution of arms. Rising in Barcelona and Madrid defeated.
20 July	General Sanjurjo dies in an air crash in Portugal.
30 July	Nine Savoia-Marchetti S.81 bombers, out of the twelve sent by Mussolini, reach Morocco.
2 August	Léon Blum proposes the policy of non-intervention.
8 August	France closes its border with Spain.
12 August	The first volunteers of the International Brigades reach Spain.
14 August	Badajoz falls to the Army of Africa.
24 August	Franco's international backers – Germany, Italy and Portugal – accept the principles of non-intervention.
26 August	Popular tribunals created by the Republican government.
4 September	Popular Front government created under Largo Caballero.
5 September	Irun falls to General Mola, who closes off the land links between the Republic's northern zone (Basque Country and Asturias) and France.
7 September	An autonomous Basque government is formed for the first time.
9 September	First meeting of the Non-Intervention Committee in London.

26 September	CNT joins the Generalitat Council.
27 September	Relief of the Alcázar in Toledo.
29 September	Franco becomes head of state with the tacit agreement of the army.
1 October	Basque autonomy approved by the Cortes.
12 October	First arrival of Soviet aid for the Republic.
4 November	CNT enters the Spanish government.
6 November	Republican government leaves Madrid for Valencia.
7 November	Battle for Madrid begins.
18 November	Germany and Italy recognize the Nationalists as the legitimate power in Spain.
20 November	Deaths of Durrutti in Madrid and José Antonio Primo de Rivera in Alicante.
23 November	Battle for Madrid ends.
17 December	POUM removed from the Council of the Generalitat.
22 December	First Italian troops arrive in Cadiz.

1937

6 January	USA forbids the export of arms to Spain.
5 February	Battle of the Jarama begins.
7 February	Malaga falls to a joint Nationalist–Italian offensive.
8 March	Battle of Guadalajara begins.
30 March	Mola launches offensive against the Basque Country.
19 April	Unification of Falange and Carlists in a single party (FET y de las JONS) with Franco as its leader. Land and sea verification procedures established around Spain in order to enforce the principles of non-intervention.
26 April	Guernica bombed by the Condor Legion.
3 May	May Days begin in Barcelona.
17 May	Negrín appointed prime minister.
16 June	POUM dissolved.
19 June	Bilbao falls.
6 July	Brunete offensive – first of the new Popular Army – launched.
10 August	Council of Aragon dissolved by the Republican government.
24 August	Aragon offensive launched by the Popular Army.
26 August	Santander captured by the Nationalists.
28 August	The Holy See recognizes the Nationalist regime.

19 October	War in the north comes to an end as Gijón is captured by the Nationalists.
29 October	Republican government moves to Barcelona.
14 December	Popular Army launches offensive in the Teruel sector.

1938

30 January	Franco turns the Junta Técnica del Estado into a government.
22 February	Teruel recaptured by Franco's forces.
10 March	Nationalist offensive launched in Aragon.
17 March	Blum momentarily reopens Franco-Spanish border.
14 April	Nationalist army reaches the Mediterranean, cutting the Republican zone in two.
1 May	Juan Negrín announces the Thirteen Points package of war aims.
24 July	Ebro offensive by the Popular Army brings the Nationalist drive on Valencia to a halt.
22 September	International Brigades withdrawn from the battle areas and then from Spain.
16 November	Popular Army withdraws across the Ebro.
23 December	Nationalist drive on Catalonia begins.

1939

26 January	Barcelona falls to the Nationalists.
1 February	Last meeting of the Cortes on Spanish soil, in the border town of Figueras.
9 February	Franco issues the Law of Political Responsibilities.
27 February	France and Great Britain recognize the Franco government. Azaña, in France, resigns as president of the Republic.
5 March	Council of National Defence, headed by Colonel Casado, launches a coup in Madrid.
6 March	Negrín leaves Spain for the last time.
24 March	The Council's representatives attempt to negotiate a surrender with the Nationalists, but their terms are rejected on Franco's orders.
27 March	Franco captures Madrid.
1 April	Franco declares victory.

Personalities

Aguirre, José Antonio (1904–60) Basque nationalist who led the first home rule government in the region, established in October 1936. At odds with the Valencia government over the treatment of the Catholic Church in the Republic and over the military conduct of the war. After the capture of the Basque Country the Basque government fled first to Catalonia, and then abroad, Aguirre preserving his title until his death.

Alcalá Zamora, Niceto (1877–1949) Minister of public works in 1917, and minister of war in 1922, served as the first prime minister of the Second Republic in 1931, resigning in December of that year in protest at the government's anticlerical measures. Elected president of the Second Republic, serving from December 1931 until his removal from office by the Cortes in 1936. Exiled in France and Argentina.

Alvarez del Vayo, Julio (1891–1974) Socialist who served as foreign minister from September 1936 to May 1937, and from April 1938 until the end of the Civil War. Close to the PCE, he directed his efforts unsuccessfully at the League of Nations.

Ascaso, Joaquín (?–1939) Anarchist president of the Council of Aragon, established in 1936. Pursued the collectivization of agriculture only to find agricultural and mining output down on pre-war figures. Discredited by a communist-led campaign, he was dismissed in August 1937 and arrested.

Azaña, Manuel (1880–1940) Leading political figure of the Second Republic. Established the Acción Republicana party in 1930;

served as minister of war in 1931 and prime minister from 1931 to 1933. Arrested in 1934 under suspicion of collusion with the October rising in Catalonia, campaigned tirelessly for the establishment of a Popular Front government in 1936. Served briefly as prime minister in 1936, and as president from 1936 to 1939. Died in exile in France.

Besteiro, Julián (1870–1940) Socialist politician and Professor of Philosophy at the University of Madrid. Served as president of the UGT, and was elected deputy in all three Republican elections. At the very right of the PSOE, he was gradually pushed out of the political scene by Largo Caballero. A pacifist, Besteiro did not become involved in the war effort, apart from some failed mediation attempts. Joined Casado's coup, but refused to leave Madrid in the face of the Nationalist advance. Arrested, he was sentenced to thirty years' imprisonment and died in jail soon after.

Calvo Sotelo, José (1893–1936) Right-wing politician who served as Primo de Rivera's finance minister. Exiled in 1931, he was amnestied in 1934. Upon his return to Spain Calvo Sotelo took over the Renovación Española party, becoming the most significant opposition figure in 1936. His murder on 13 July 1936 was used as a justification for the military rising that followed.

Casado, Segismundo (1893–1968) Military officer who remained loyal to the Republic. Served as chief of staff during the Brunete offensive, and was commander of the Central Zone by late 1938. Led a rising in Madrid against the Negrín government in March 1939, but the subsequent failure to negotiate a truce with Franco forced him to seek exile in Britain. He returned to Spain in the 1960s.

Companys, Lluys (1883–1940) Catalan nationalist who was first elected to the Cortes in 1921. First speaker of the Catalan parliament during the Republic, he was elected president of the Generalitat in January 1934. He proclaimed the existence of a Catalan state in October 1934, and was arrested as a result. President of the Generalitat again in 1936, Companys collaborated with the CNT after the military rising but saw his influence decline in the aftermath of the May Days. Exiled in France, he was arrested by the Gestapo and returned to Spain where he was executed.

Durruti, Buenaventura (1896–1936) Member of the famous Solidarios anarchist group, responsible for the murder of the Archbishop of Zaragoza in 1923. Lived in exile in France and South America, returning to Spain to lead revolts against the Republic. Commanded an armed column in Aragon in 1936, failing to capture Zaragoza, and in Madrid, where he died in confused circumstances.

Gil Robles, José Maria (1901–80) Leader of the CEDA, was discredited among right-wing circles for his failure to hold on to power in 1936. Although he supported financially the military rising, Gil Robles was shunned by the Nationalist camp and forced to leave Spain. He would later work against the Franco regime, supporting the establishment of a constitutional monarchy.

Giral, José (1880–1962) Republican politician and Professor of Chemistry who served as navy minister from 1931 to 1933 and again in 1936. Prime minister from July to September 1936, leading an all-republican cabinet which failed to restore order. Foreign Minister briefly in 1937.

González, Valentín (?–1965) Communist militiaman turned officer who was nicknamed 'El Campesino'. Shot to prominence in the fighting in the Sierra north of Madrid in 1936, and was then involved in most important battles of the war. Controversially ordered the execution of 400 Moroccan prisoners of war in retaliation for earlier Nationalist atrocities. Lived in exile in the USSR and later in France.

Ibárruri, Dolores (1895–1981) Communist Party member, better known as La Pasionaria. She was noted for her propaganda efforts during the Civil War both in Spain – notably in the defence of Madrid – and abroad. President of the PCE in exile, La Pasionaria was elected to the Cortes in 1977.

Largo Caballero, Francisco (1869–1946) Socialist politician and trade-union leader who was sentenced to life imprisonment for his role in the 1917 general strike. He was elected to the Cortes the following year and therefore released. Largo collaborated with the Primo de Rivera dictatorship, and then served as labour minister from 1931 to 1933. He supported the 1934 rising, and was again arrested following its failure. Largo was the first socialist prime minister in Spain, leading a Popular Front government from September 1936 to May 1937. Exiled in France, he was sent by the Nazis to Dachau concentration camp but survived.

Lerroux, Alejandro (1864–1949) Radical politician who was first elected to the Cortes in 1901. Served as foreign minister in 1931. His importance rose after the 1933 elections, leading a number of cabinets from 1933 until 1935. A serious financial scandal and the polarization of politics in the 1936 election led to an electoral debacle. Lerroux was in exile until 1947, despite having supported Franco during the Civil War.

Martínez Barrio, Diego (1883–1962) Republican politician who served as prime minister and minister of the interior in 1933. He became speaker of the Cortes in 1936 and was prime minister briefly in July 1936, only to find that his intended policy of negotiation with the military rebels was impossible to carry out. Martínez Barrio was in exile from 1939, taking over the title of president from Azaña and keeping it until his death.

Miaja, José (1878–1958) Military officer who remained loyal to the Republic, despite earlier membership of the UME. He accepted the post of war minister under Martínez Barrio, but not Giral. Miaja was named to lead the defence of Madrid despite earlier defeats. Success saw him elevated to heroic status by the Communist Party. Joined Casado in the National Council of Defence in 1939.

Mola, Emilio (1887–1937) Born in Cuba, he served in Morocco before becoming director general of security in the Berenguer dictatorship in 1930. Mola was nicknamed El Director for his planning of the military rising of 1936. During the Civil War he commanded the Army of the North in 1936 and 1937, dying that year in an aeroplane crash.

Negrín, Juan (1889–1956) Socialist politician and Professor of Physiology at the University of Madrid. He was elected to the Cortes in all three Republican elections, remaining a back-bencher. During the Civil War Negrín served first as finance minister from September 1936 to May 1937 and then as prime minister until the end of the conflict, keeping the title until 1945. After the Civil War he lived in exile in France, Britain and the USA.

Nin, Andrés (1892–1937) Member of the CNT and the PCE, Nin broke with Stalin in 1931, forming his own Marxist party, the POUM, with Catalonia as a power base. He was briefly a member of the Generalitat in 1936. Arrested after the May Days, Nin was sent in June to a Soviet-run detention camp at Alcalá de Henares, where he was killed.

Prieto, Indalecio (1883–1962) Socialist politician first elected to the Cortes in 1918. Prieto served as minister of finance and of public works under the Republic, participating in the 1934 rising but fleeing into exile after its failure. A reformist, he was concerned with establishing a progressive bloc of socialists and republicans. Prevented by Largo Caballero from becoming prime minister in 1936, Prieto served during the Civil War as navy and air force minister under Largo Caballero, and national defence minister under Negrín until March 1938. He remained active in socialist politics in exile until his death, conducting a violent polemic with Negrín.

Primo de Rivera, José Antonio (1903–1936) Eldest son of Miguel Primo de Rivera who was driven by the desire to clear his father's name. He founded the Falange and was elected to the Cortes in 1933, losing his seat in 1936. The Falange's participation in street violence led to his arrest that year. Primo de Rivera authorized the Falange's participation in the military rising. He was executed in November 1936, but was subsequently elevated to the status of martyr by Franco, and his writings became official doctrine for the Spanish state.

Queipo de Llano, Gonzalo (1875–1951) Military officer and *africanista* whose disagreements with Miguel Primo de Rivera led to a brief jail term. In April 1936 he was appointed director general of the Carabineros. Queipo de Llano was related by the marriage of their children to Niceto Alcalá Zamora, which damaged his credibility among the Nationalists. He captured the city of Seville in 1936 at the head of a mere 200 men, and then commanded the Army of the South. Famous for his outrageous wartime broadcasts, he attempted to rule southern Spain, introducing economic reforms.

Rojo, Vicente (1894–1966) Military officer who remained loyal to the Republic, despite not having obvious political leanings. Rojo developed the strategy for the defence of Madrid and numerous other battles from Guadalajara to the Ebro. He lived in exile after the war, returning to Spain in 1958.

Sanjurjo, José (1887–1937) Army officer nicknamed the 'Lion of the Rif' for his participation in the Moroccan fighting. Director of the Guardia Civil in 1931, Sanjurjo pledged its loyalty to the Republic. He was nevertheless demoted to the Carabineros, which in turn motivated his 1932 coup. Arrested and sentenced to death, Sanjurjo's sentence was commuted and he received an amnesty in 1934, finding exile in Portugal. His Carlist connections facilitated the conspiratorial task of Emilio Mola, who invited him to lead the military rising. Sanjurjo accepted, but died while trying to return to Spain.

Yagüe, Juan (1891–1952) Military officer and *africanista* who was involved in the repression of the Asturian rising in 1934. A leading conspirator in Morocco in 1936, seizing Ceuta, Yagüe was politically close to the Falange. As commander of the Army of Africa in the early stages of the war Yagüe met with great success, but he failed to take Madrid. He led the Moroccan corps in Teruel and in the Aragon offensive, capturing the Catalan city of Lérida, but expressed disagreement with Franco in 1938, for which he was punished. Yagüe was rehabilitated in time to participate in the Ebro Battle.

Bibliography

GENERAL WORKS

Aguilar Fernández, P. (1996) *Memoria y Olvido de la Guerra Española*. Madrid: Alianza Editorial.

Carr, R. (1982) *Spain 1808–1975* (2nd edn). Oxford: Clarendon.

Carr, R. (1993) *The Spanish Tragedy: The Civil War in Perspective*. London: Weidenfeld.

Cortada, J. (1982) *Historical Dictionary of the Spanish Civil War*. London: Greenwood Press.

Esenwein, G.R. and Shubert, A. (1995) *Spain at War: The Spanish Civil War in Context, 1931–1939*. London: Longman.

Fraser, R. (1994) *Blood of Spain: An Oral History of the Spanish Civil War*. London: Pimlico.

Graham, H. and Labanyi, J. (eds) (1995) *Spanish Cultural Studies: An Introduction*. Oxford: Oxford University Press.

Jackson, G. (1965) *The Spanish Republic and the Civil War, 1931–39*. Princeton: Princeton University Press.

Lannon, F. (1987) *Privilege, Persecution, and Prophecy: The Catholic Church in Spain 1875–1975*. Oxford: Clarendon.

Madariaga, S. (1961) *Spain: A Modern History*. London: Jonathan Cape.

Preston, P. (1988) 'The legacy of the Spanish Civil War', in Hart, S.M. (ed.), *op. cit.*, pp. 11–19.

Preston, P. (1996a) *A Concise History of the Spanish Civil War*. London: Fontana.

Preston, P. (ed.) (1984) *Revolution and War in Spain 1931–1939*. London: Methuen.

Preston, P. and Mackenzie, A.L. (eds) (1996) *The Republic Besieged: Civil War in Spain, 1936–1939*. Edinburgh: Edinburgh University Press.

Shubert, A. (1990) *A Social History of Modern Spain*. London: Unwin Hyman.

Smith, A. and Mal-Molinero, C. (eds) (1996) *Nationalism and National Identities in the Iberian Peninsula*. Oxford: Berg.

Thomas, Hugh (1977) *The Spanish Civil War* (3rd edn). Harmondsworth: Penguin.

ORIGINS OF THE WAR

Balfour, S. '"The lion and the pig": Nationalism and national identity in *fin-de-siècle* Spain'. See Smith and Mal Molinero, *op. cit.*, pp. 97–117.

Ben-Ami, S. (1983) *Fascism from Above: the Dictatorship of Primo de Rivera in Spain, 1923–1930*. Oxford: Clarendon.

Blinkhorn, M. (1975) *Carlism and Crisis in Spain, 1931–9*. Cambridge: Cambridge University Press.

Brenan, G. (1993) *The Spanish Labyrinth: An Account of the Social and Political Background of the Spanish Civil War*. Cambridge: Cambridge University Press.

Meaker, G. (1974) *The Revolutionary Left in Spain, 1914–23*. Stanford: Stanford University Press.

Peers, E.A. (1936) *The Spanish Tragedy* (2nd edn). London: Methuen.

Preston, P. (1994) *The Coming of the Spanish Civil War: Reform, Reaction and Revolution in the Second Republic*. London: Routledge.

Radcliff, P.B. (1996) *From Mobilization to Civil War: The Politics of Polarization in the Spanish City of Gijón, 1900–1937*. Cambridge: Cambridge University Press.

WARTIME PUBLICATIONS

American League Against War and Fascism (1936) *Spain's Democracy Talks to America*. New York: American League Against War and Fascism.

Berryer (1938) *Revolutionary Justice in Spain*. London: Burns, Oates & Washbourne.

Bulletin of Spanish Studies (Liverpool).

Burns, E. (1936) *Spain*. London: Communist Party of Great Britain.

Carreras, L. (1939) *The Glory of Martyred Spain*. London: Burns, Oates & Washbourne.

Comité Mondial Contre la Guerre et le Fascisme (1938) *Les Buts Militaires de l'Allemagne et de l'Italie dans la guerre d'Espagne*. Paris.

Curran, E.L. (1937) *Franco: Who Is He? What Does He Fight For?* New York: International Catholic Truth Society.

Dallet, J. (1938) *Letters from Spain by Joe Dallet, American Volunteer, to His Wife*. New York: Workers' Library.

Dimitroff, G. (1937) *Spain and the People's Front*. New York: Workers' Library.

Dingle, R.J. (1937) *'Democracy' in Spain*. London: Burns, Oates & Washbourne.

Dingle, R.J. (1938) *Second Thoughts on 'Democracy' in Spain*. London: Burns, Oates & Washbourne.

Ercoli, M. (1936) *The Spanish Revolution*. New York: Workers' Publishers.

Federación Española de Trabajadores de la Enseñanza (1937) *Les Professionales de l'enseignement luttent pour la Libération du peuple Espagnol*.

Friends of Democracy and Independence in Spain (1938) *Italians in Spain*.

Fuller, Major General J.F.C. (1937) *The Conquest of Red Spain*. London: Burns, Oates & Washbourne.

Goebbels, J. (1937) *The Truth about Spain: Speech Delivered at the National Socialist Party Congress, Nürnberg, 1937*. Berlin: Müller & Son.

Gwynne, H.A. and Ramos Oliveira, A. (1938) *Controversy on Spain*. London: United Editorial.

Hericourt, P. (1938) *Arms for Red Spain*. London: Burns, Oates & Washbourne.

Jerrold, D. (1937) *Spain: Impressions and Reflections*. London: Constable.

Keep the Spanish Embargo Committee (n.d.) *Keep the Spanish Embargo!* Washington, DC: National Council of Catholic Men.

La Tragédie Espagnole: Conférence donnée au Théatre des Ambassadeurs le mercredi 27 Avril 1938.

Lunn, A. (1937) *The Unpopular Front*. London: Burns, Oates & Washbourne.
Marty, A. (1937) *Heroic Spain*. New York: Workers' Library.
McNeill-Moss, Major G. (1937) *The Legend of Badajoz*. London: Burns, Oates & Washbourne.
Permartín Sanjuán, J. (1938) *Los Orígenes del Movimiento*. Burgos: Publicaciones del Ministerio de Educación Nacional.
Sencourt, R. (1938) *Spain's Ordeal: A Documented Survey of Recent Events*. London: Longmans, Green.
Spanish Embassy in Washington, DC (1937) *Spain's War of Independence*. Washington, DC: Spanish Embassy.

PERSONAL ACCOUNTS

Abellán, J.L. (1983) *De la Guerra Civil al Exilio Republicano (1936–1977)*. Madrid: Editorial Mezquita.
Alvarez del Vayo, J. (1940) *Freedom's Battle*. London: W. Heinemann.
Azaña, M. (1990) *Obras Completas IV – Memorias Politicas y de Guerra*. Madrid: Ediciones Giner.
Azcárate, M. (1994) *Derrotas y Esperanzas: La República, la Guerra Civil y la Resistencia*. Barcelona: Tusquets Editores.
Barea, A. (1972) *The Forging of a Rebel*. London: Davis-Poynter.
Borkenau, F. (1937) *The Spanish Cockpit: An Eye-witness Account of the Political and Social Conflicts in the Spanish Civil War*. London: Faber and Faber.
Galland, A. (1957) *The First and the Last*. London: Transworld Publishers.
Ibarruri, D. (1967) *They Shall Not Pass: The Autobiography of La Pasionaria*. London: Lawrence & Wishart
Koestler, A. (1984) *The Invisible Writing: The Second Volume of an Autobiography: 1932–40*. New York: Stein and Day.
Largo Caballero, F. (1985) *Escritos de la Republica*. Madrid: Editorial Pablo Iglesias.
Prieto, I. and Negrín, J. (1990) *Epistolario Prieto–Negrín: Puntos de Vista Sobre el Desarrollo y Consequencias de la Guerra Civil Española*. Barcelona: Fundación Indalecio Prieto/Editorial Planeta.
Rodríguez Olazábal, J. (1996) *La Administración de Justicia en la Guerra Civil*. Valencia: Edicions Alfons el Magnánim.

FOREIGN INTERVENTION

Abreu, F. (1998) 'A rádio portuguesa e a guerra civil de Espanha', in Rosas, F. (ed.), *Portugal e a Guerra Civil de Espanha*. Lisbon: Edições Colibri.

Buchanan, T. (1997) *Britain and the Spanish Civil War*. Cambridge: Cambridge University Press.

Carr, E.H. and Deutscher, T. (eds) (1984) *The Comintern and the Spanish Civil War*. London: Macmillan.

McGarry, F. (1999) *Irish Politics and the Spanish Civil War*. Cork: Cork University Press.

Moradiellos, E. (1996) 'The gentle general: the official British perception of General Franco during the Spanish Civil War', in Preston, P. and Mackenzie, A.L. (eds), *op. cit.*, pp. 1–19.

Oliveira, C. (1998) *Salazar e a Guerra Civil de Espanha* (2nd edn). Lisbon: O Jornal.

Preston, P. (1996b) 'Mussolini's Spanish adventure: from limited risk to war', in Preston, P. and Mackenzie, A.L. (eds), *op. cit.*, pp. 21–51.

Veatch, R. (1990) 'The League of Nations and the Spanish Civil War, 1936–9', *European History Quarterly*, 20, 2, pp. 181–207.

THE NATIONALISTS' WAR

Ellwood, S.M. (1990) 'Falange Española and the creation of a Francoist state', *European History Quarterly*, 20, 2, pp. 209–25.

Payne, S.G. (1961) *Falange: A History of Spanish Fascism*. Stanford: Stanford University Press.

Payne, S.G. (1967) *Politics and the Military in Modern Spain*. Stanford: Stanford University Press.

Preston, P. (1990) *The Politics of Revenge: Fascism and the Military in Twentieth Century Spain*. London: Unwin Hyman.

Preston, P. (1993) *Franco: A Biography*. London: HarperCollins.

Richards, M. (1998) *A Time of Silence: Civil War and the Culture of Repression in Franco's Spain, 1936–1945*. Cambridge: Cambridge University Press.

THE REPUBLICANS' WAR

Alexander, R. (1999) *The Anarchists in the Spanish Civil War*. London: Janus.

Bolloten, B. (1961) *The Grand Camouflage: The Communist Conspiracy in the Spanish Civil War*. London: Hollis & Carter.

Broué, P. and Témine, E. (1961) *La Révolution et la Guerre d'Espagne*. Paris: Les Editions de Minuit.

Corbin, J.R. (1993) *The Anarchist Passion: Class Conflict in Southern Spain 1810–1965*. Aldershot: Avebury.

Ealham, C. (1996) '"From the summit to the abyss": the contradictions of individualism and collectivization in Spanish Anarchism', in Preston, P. and Mackenzie, A.L. (eds), *op. cit.*, pp. 135–62.

Graham, H. (1991) *Socialism and War: The Spanish Socialist Party in Power and Crisis, 1936–1939*. Cambridge: Cambridge University Press.

Graham, H. (1996a) 'War, modernity and reform: the premiership of Juan Negrín 1937–1939', in Preston, P. and Mackenzie, A.L. (eds), *op. cit.*, pp. 163–96.

Graham, H. (1996b) 'Community, nation and the state in Republican Spain, 1931–1938', in Smith, A. and Mal-Molinero, C. (eds), *op. cit.*, pp. 133–47.

Graham, H. (1999) 'Against the state: a genealogy of the Barcelona May Days (1937)', *European History Quarterly*, 29, 4, pp. 485–542.

Kurzman, D. (1980) *Miracle of November: Madrid's Epic Stand, 1936*. New York: G.P. Putnam's Sons.

Seidman, M. (1990) 'The Unorwellian Barcelona', *European History Quarterly*, 20, 2, pp. 163–80.

POPULAR MOBILIZATION

Díaz-Plaja, F. (1994) *La Vida Cotidiana en la España de la Guerra Civil*. Madrid: Edaf.

Glendinning, N. (1988) 'Art and the Spanish Civil War', in Hart, S.M. (ed.), *op. cit.*, pp. 20–45.

Hart, S.M. (ed.) (1988) *'No Pasarán': Art, Literature and the Spanish Civil War*. London: Tamesis Books.

Heinemann, M. (1988) 'English poetry and the war in Spain: some records of a generation', in Hart, S.M. (ed.), *op. cit.*, pp. 46–64.

Kenwood, A. (ed.) (1993) *The Spanish Civil War: A Cultural and Historical Reader*. Oxford: Berg.

Lewis, T. (1988) '"L'Espoir": André Malraux and the art of propaganda', in Hart, S.M. (ed.), *op. cit.*, pp. 83–105.

Low, R. (1992) *La Pasionaria: The Spanish Firebrand.* London: Hutchinson.

Mangini, S. (1995) *Memories of Resistance: Women's Voices from the Spanish Civil War.* New Haven: Yale University Press.

Monteath, P. (1994) *Writing the Good Fight: Political Commitment in the International Literature of the Spanish Civil War.* London: Greenwood Press.

Index

143